# A CUP OF COMFORT®
# for
# Fathers

Stories that celebrate
everything we love about Dad

Edited by
Colleen Sell

**A**damsmedia

Avon, Massachusetts

*For my extraordinary father,*
*Albert Sell*

A *Cup of Comfort*® is a registered trademark of F+W Media, Inc.

Published by
Adams Media, a division of F+W Media, Inc.
57 Littlefield Street, Avon, MA 02322 U.S.A.
*www.adamsmedia.com* and *www.cupofcomfort.com*

ISBN 10: 1-60550-090-9
ISBN 13: 978-1-60550-090-4

Printed in the United States of America.

10 9 8 7 6 5 4 3 2 1

**Library of Congress Cataloging-in-Publication Data**
is available from the publisher.

*This book is available at quantity discounts for bulk purchases.*
*For information, please call 1-800-289-0963.*

# Contents

# Acknowledgments

Top billing and a standing ovation go to my dad, Albert Sell. His unconditional love for, unfailing dedication to, and unbridled pride and joy in his children set the gold standard for fatherhood. He is my rock and my soft place to fall, my guiding light and my champion.

My sincere appreciation goes to all of the authors who submitted their personal stories for publication consideration in this book.

A round of applause and my deepest gratitude go to the authors whose stories grace these pages.

As always, my thanks go to the extraordinary team at Adams Media—especially Meredith O'Hayre, the director of this ensemble piece.

And thank you, dear readers, for giving us an audience for these wonderful stories.

# Introduction

*"It's only when you grow up, and step back
from him, or leave him for your own career
and your own home—it's only then that
you can measure his greatness and fully
appreciate it. Pride reinforces love."*

—Margaret Truman

Growing up, I thought my dad was the cat's meow.
The bravest, smartest, funniest, strongest, kindest,
sweetest, bestest dad in the world. Handsome too.
And he could fix anything, from bikes to boo-boos
to broken hearts. But I didn't fully recognize what a
great man and extraordinary father he was, and is,
until I became an adult and had children of my own.
Then, every sacrifice he'd made, every heroic deed

he'd done, every lesson he'd taught, and every act of love he'd given became crystal clear to me. And I realized just how blessed I really am.

That's when I also realized, to my surprise, that not every father is as present and accounted for in their children's lives as my dad has always been. *You mean,* I'd think to myself when I'd learn of a less hands-on father than mine, *your dad didn't read to you and tuck you in at night? Didn't change diapers, wipe runny noses, and give baths? Didn't get down on the floor or go out in the backyard and play with you, really play with you? Didn't take you to dancing lessons and ballgames and museums and parks and on family vacations? Didn't talk with (not at) you, didn't consider your opinion, didn't ask how you felt? Didn't help you with your homework, build your Soapbox Derby car, move into your first place, or sort through a tough situation? Didn't shower you with kisses and hugs and "way to gos"?*

Of course, my dad was hands-on before hands-on was cool. Men of his generation weren't expected to interact with, and enjoy, their kids as much as my dad did. But Dad had a great role model who was ahead of his time, too: his own father (of fourteen, no less). My brothers have continued their legacy, and I am confident the future fathers in our family will too.

My son has often said, "I want to be the man and father my grandpa is." Every time, I've smiled and assured him that he could have no better role model . . . and felt guilty and sad because the man I chose to be my children's father has had a peripheral, rather than a central role, in their lives.

Still, my children love and respect their father, as well they should. They value and cherish their relationships with him, even as they've longed for more time and a deeper connection with him. And, as my thirty-two-year-old son discovered this summer, it is never too late to strengthen, or create, that father-child bond. Recently, after thirty years of feeling disconnected from his father, of feeling that he didn't really know his dad and that his dad didn't really know him, my son drove from Oregon to Arizona for a two-week visit with his dad. It was the first time they'd spent time alone together, just the two of them, since Mickey was a toddler. And they connected, really connected. And got to know each other, man to man. Their time together strengthened the bond between them and deepened their love and respect for one another. That is something to celebrate!

*A Cup of Comfort for Fathers*® is filled with stories that celebrate fatherhood and that honor fathers of all persuasions—new dads, super dads, divorced dads, stay-at-home dads, stepdads, and hands-on dads like mine.

Enjoy!

*A Cup of Comfort for Fathers*® is filled with stories that celebrate fatherhood and that honor fathers of all persuasions—new dads, super dads, divorced dads, stay-at-home dads, stepdads, and hands-on dads like mine.

Enjoy!

—*Colleen Sell*

# A Few Minutes
# in the Shade

I have a son. He's five. About three times a week since he was an infant, I have given him a bath. It's been a gauge as to the passage of time.

When he first came home, all tiny, red, and premature, it was a struggle. He cried and wiggled and tried to get away. I tried not to lose my grip; he was so slippery.

Then he got a little bigger, and we graduated to the kitchen sink and that blue monster of a baby bathtub. He enjoyed it, as did I.

He continued to grow and we moved into the "big" bathtub. I was more scared than he was, always trying to make sure he didn't drown. Every bath was an adventure.

Then my daughter was born, and her baths renewed the cycle: the fear of losing my grip, the kitchen sink, the blue monster, the "big bathtub." My son watched it all . . . and wanted toys. He got his sister.

They get along well and always have. The year and a half they took baths together was a joy. Splashing and crying, slipping and falling. But most of all playing—first with each other, then with their toys, then with Mom and me.

Then it was apparent that the time for shared baths was over. Biology began to be noticed. They got too big. They wanted to take baths "by myself."

And so it goes . . .

About three times a week (as my schedule allows), I give them a bath.

My son is five. He knows everything (and is more than willing to tell it to you). Yet, he wants to know more. He wants to know it all.

I've come to treasure our time together in the bath. It's when we talk, just me and my son. We talk about everything and nothing. We talk about things that happen in school (kindergarten is full of adventures). We talk about life. We sing songs. He asks me questions. I answer them as best I can. I ask him questions. He answers in a way his dad can understand (nothing too complicated, you know).

Lately, when we're finished talking and singing and discussing the great mysteries of life, when we are finished soaping up and washing hair and rinsing off, my son, who is five, asks me if he can just "take a few minutes in the shade." When I tell him that he can, he lies back in the bath water, reclining against the back of the tub submerged to his neck as the water drains out. I asked him, "What does it mean to 'take a few minutes in the shade'?"

He answered me very solemnly, not wanting to show his disappointment. His dad didn't know.

"It means to take a break, to relax before you have to go back out there," he said, pointing to the bathroom door.

Recently, I have found myself explaining to a room full of grown children that their mother is certain to die soon. And how important it is to allow her to do so in dignity.

I have sat and laughed with a man as we conspired to see how long he could go before his emphysema drives him back to the manacle of plastic and steel, his oxygen tank.

I have cried with a young woman with severe chronic asthma as she realized that she will take medications every day of her life. That she will die at a young age. That she will not live to see her five-year-old daughter grow up.

I have resuscitated a young woman with metastatic bone cancer, who had a "do not resuscitate" order. Lifted her off the floor, intubated, and forced life back into her. It was not her time. Her husband and daughters had not said their goodbyes yet.

I have lectured a teenage girl who tried to commit suicide not to throw away her life. Seeing in her blank expression the loneliness and despair of her life, I turned and walked out of the room, vowing that my daughter will always be loved, that she will never feel that death is her only friend.

"I'll do it again," said the girl with the blank expression.

I have sat vigil with a man with amyotrophic lateral sclerosis (ALS), Lou Gehrig's disease, after I removed the ventilator so that he could die a natural death, at his request. I watched him gasp for air. Gave him morphine to make him comfortable. Answered his family's questions as he lay dying for four hours. I listened as he took his last breath, and then closed his eyes. I said the Lord's Prayer with his family and hugged his mother as I walked out of the room.

I have heard my partner on the phone arguing with an HMO. They refused to pay for a lymphoma patient's last three days on a ventilator. His widow was going to have to pay. "He died anyway, so it wasn't necessary," they said.

I am dealing with a system that will not pay to do an electrocardiogram on someone with chest pain in my office but will pay to rule out myocardial infarction at the hospital.

I struggle daily to scrape together samples of medications for my patients. They have coverage for the doctor but not for pharmaceuticals. They have no money for medications. They cost too much. So they take half of what they should (or less) and hope for the best.

Tonight, though, I am in luck.

I get to go home and be with my family. And I will give my son a bath.

He is five.

And we'll talk about school. We'll talk about when his birthday is, and why it's getting dark earlier, and does the Earth really go around the sun? We'll sing silly songs about silly things. He'll change the words to make the songs even sillier. And we'll laugh.

When the washing and singing and rinsing are all done and I say that it's time to get out of the bath, he will ask if he can "take just a few minutes in the shade."

Tonight, I will look at him, memorize his every expression, hold it in my mind and heart. And I'll say, "Sure, we'll both take a few minutes in the shade."

Then we'll both take a break and relax . . . before we have to go back out there.

—*Pedro H. Calves, MD*

# Alchemy

Julian has a laboratory in the backyard. Be careful! You have to step carefully; you don't want to disrupt one of the dozens of cups he has so carefully positioned. Inside the containers are potentially dangerous "potions," as he calls them. For example, he has been working on a "chlorine explosure" mixture. No doubt its effects are quite deadly.

I consider this activity to be a form of the ancient science of alchemy, but whatever you call it, my five-year-old son's potion-making has placed our kitchen—especially the spice shelf—in a constant state of disruption. He uses, of course, the customary elements for this age-old activity: grass, leaves, mud, sticks, worms, whatever. But he also adds scads of spices and other foodstuffs. I count no less than nine cups and glasses of potions. Four larger containers, a pie pan, a Tupperware bowl, a plastic jug, and a silver teapot round out his wares.

The blond boy toils, his face fastened in concentration upon his task, cheek pierced by a dimple. His attention is unwavering as he pours a cupful of magic potion into a bowl, a pinch of the teapot's contents into the glass jar, a dollop of the coffee mug mixture into the plastic jug. The pie pan is the ultimate cauldron, the place where everything else is finally poured, and Julian always adds one briquette of charcoal to the pie-pan potion to, as he puts it, "give it some kick."

He demonstrates his technique for me at the kitchen table. A number of cups and glasses are on the table, vessels ready for alchemical preparations. Into a plastic cup Julian mixes the following: paprika, basil, garlic powder, oregano, sassafras, and tea. He's singing the name of each ingredient as he pours or taps it into the cup—though some of the items are unknown to him. The smells are of course important in identifying each substance, and he cautions: the hot spices "burn like ka-joosious if it gets in your eye."

I want to throttle him when pulls an egg out of the refrigerator to break into the cup. But I don't. I remember well this urge to engage in alchemy. As a child, I would take a frying pan into the backyard and toss all sorts of organic matter into it. I recall a profound feeling of imminent magic: I truly believed

I was going to create life. What form that life might take I'm not sure I ever visualized, but I would sit in my backyard for hours stirring this primordial soup.

The egg, Julian admits, doesn't do much, except make it "sticky." He continues his soprano trill, mixing dill, golden seal, vanilla, soy sauce, and milk into another cup. One small spice container he calls "chicken juice," because there's a picture of dinner-ready turkey on the label. It's poultry seasoning, a new spice on me. I ask him what this particular potion is going to be.

"Suck-oh-lee-lu-lee-lu," he announces. Then, sensing my confusion, he clarifies: "That's Spanish talk for poisonous fish killer."

I ask him what fish he intends on poisoning, but he doesn't answer. He's too busy adding cinnamon to all of his present potions. Julian is obsessed with cinnamon; he uses it in his laboratory as well as on his toast. He shakes the powder into each of his cups.

Recently, he's also been developing a "Katie Hoover sickness potion." Julian is hell-bent on giving her some kind of illness. It seems she was responsible for a firestorm of criticism at school regarding his new haircut.

He tells me that he knows a potion is finished when "Mr. Lungs goes ERRRR!" This must be a reference to the pulmonary reaction that occurs when the combination of spices reaches critical mass. Sure enough, a few moments after the cinnamon sift, his little Mr. Lungs scream out, and so we know the formula is ready.

I follow him outside as he sets the cup among the others. It's a crisp, sunny day, well on the way to winter. Despite the cold, Julian wears nothing but a pair of black shorts. Fallen leaves crackle beneath our feet, and I can see that a few leaves have volunteered themselves into the various vessels. Julian begins pouring the cups into the pie pan, reciting incantations like a seasoned alchemist.

The practice of alchemy flourished for some seventeen hundred years, though many believe the discipline is much older in Asia and China. Mircea Eliade talks about the "extreme antiquity" of alchemy, born in the metallurgy and mining of ancient history. Alchemy's purpose was many-fold, though the basic quest was the transmutation of base metals into gold. Alchemists, especially those in the East, were also in search of medicinal magic to sustain youth and cure diseases.

Gold looked like the fast train to immortality. Eliade explains in his *The Forge and the Crucible* that the existing belief system, especially in China, held that all metals, when left alone long enough, would eventually turn into gold. He calls this the "natural metamorphosis of metals." The alchemist's task, then, was to transmutate these metals, speeding up

Almighty Time in the process. Depending on the procedure used, an alchemist could hope to get to the gold in the course of a few days.

No one, it seems, ever did. And that's made many people wonder why alchemy persisted for millennia. Carl Jung, in his *Psychology and Alchemy*, believed that alchemy was a process of psychological projection. The alchemist, according to Jung, was actually toiling away on his own psyche, individuating and evolving, as he mixed the chemicals before him. As Eliade puts it, Jung "was investigating the structure and behavior of the psyche" by studying alchemy.

The tactics alchemists used are mostly unknown to us. "*Obscurum per obscurious*" was their catchphrase, which Jung translates as "explaining the obscure by the more obscure." Julian would translate *obscurum per obscurious* with something more like "suck-oh-lee-lu-lee-lu." The alchemist's secrecy makes sense. A lack of exact information would come in handy whether they were triumphant or complete failures.

Were they in any way successful? In the classic work *The Golden Bough*, Sir James George Frazer says that magic, "by investigating the causal sequences of nature, directly prepares the way for science." And so modern chemistry owes much to alchemy. Jung's main premise of *Psychology and Alchemy* is that alchemy also contributed greatly to the science of psychology.

Today, if you can convince the guys at your friendly neighborhood cyclotron to take a break and have some fun, they might be able to make you a little gold. Using their handy-dandy particle accelerator, the cyclotron people can bombard lead and knock out three protons and seven neutrons . . . and presto! Gold is produced. The process is more costly than the product, but at least the ancient alchemists can rest peacefully in their graves.

Julian, at this point, is about as far away from the technology of a particle accelerator as you can get. At present, he's squatting in the backyard, finding an AWOL hair from his head and placing it into the Tupperware bowl. Absorbed, he stirs the potion with a wooden spoon.

The alchemists used hair. They also occasionally urinated into their own elixirs. I'm not going to ask, but I wouldn't be surprised if Julian takes an occasional whiz into his. In his quest to create magical potions in the backyard, Julian has stumbled—or intrinsically danced—into numerous parallels with the alchemist masters.

Take eggs, for example, one of Julian's favorite ingredients. His justification for the egg, as I've noted, is that it makes the potions sticky, but eggs are also a rich image for the alchemist, "an archetypal symbol of unity, of growth, incubation, of nature's miraculous hatching of chicks from seemingly inanimate matter"—so describes Mark Haeffner in his *Dictionary of Alchemy*.

Julian's remark that charcoal gives his potion "kick" is well-grounded in alchemical tradition. Fire is an essential element in their process, as cooking their elixirs is integral to creating gold. Charcoal is the closest Julian can get to making fire without anyone's help. With my help, he delights in lighting birthday candles, parading them out the door, then extinguishing them with a hissing flourish into one of his mixtures.

And Julian's ubiquitous use of cinnamon dovetails, in color and etymological root, with the alchemists' predilection for cinnabar. Cinnabar, when heated, releases the powerful, transformative fumes of mercury—an absolute must for the alchemist.

Julian has never mentioned gold as his goal, but he did recently recommend one of his potions "if you want your skin to never grow old." He, too, then, is creating an elixir of immortality.

For all I know, he'll find that fountain of youth someday. For now, I'll simply take the gift of never forgetting this golden image of my son in his backyard laboratory, where magic happens and anything is possible.

—*Jim Poyser*

# A Mighty Soul

I t is late morning on a sun-soaked Saturday in May. I finish packing sandwiches, chocolate chip cookies, and juice boxes into a plastic grocery bag. I saunter to the playroom and announce to our three kids, "Let's go, guys, it's time to join your brother for a picnic!"

They shriek with excitement, scurry to put on socks and shoes, negotiate our creaky screen door (*Squeak, SLAM! Squeak, SLAM! Squeak, SLAM!*), and sprint to the car. As they wedge themselves cheek-by-jowl in the back seat, Abby—the eldest at six years old and the clear ringleader of the trio— asks, "You got everything, Dad? Even the cookies?"

I nod. Luke, our youngest and Abby's enthusiastic minion, requires confirmation: "You 'member the cookies, Dad?"

"Yes," I assure him.

Daniel, their brother with mild autism, seems satisfied and silently peers out the window wearing a thin smile on his face. We begin the brief journey to visit the older brother they've never met. I glance in the rear-view mirror and see Abby concentrating.

"Dad, tell us again about Samuel. I kinda forget some parts."

*It's another sunny Saturday morning nearly eight years ago. Krista, my wife, is five months pregnant and experiencing an unusual pressure in her abdomen, accompanied by a clear discharge. She's noticeably worried, but I'm confident she's overreacting. We go to the local hospital, where she's examined and given an abdominal ultrasound.*

*A couple of hours later Krista's obstetrician approaches, looking ashen. "I'm so sorry," she mutters. She's close to tears. "It doesn't look good. You have what's known as an incompetent cervix, Krista. The musculature of your cervix wasn't able to contain the baby and the amniotic sac has begun to slough out of the cervical opening. The chances are high that he's going to be born quite early, so we need to rush you to a hospital with a high-level neonatal intensive care unit."*

*I detect that she feels our baby—we've already named him Samuel—is not going to make it.*

*Krista is placed in an ambulance, which speeds to a tertiary care facility several miles away. When we arrive, a series of nurses attend to her, taking vitals and generally issuing an air of competence. The perinatologist performs another inspection. He is gentle and calming, and I can tell he's dealt with this kind of situation many times.*

*"Okay," he begins. "You have three options right now. One: you can throw in the towel. Two: you can let me try to push the sac back in and insert a stitch in your cervix, tying it shut like a purse-string. There is a serious risk of perforating the sac during the procedure and of otherwise inducing premature labor inadvertently. Your child is only twenty or twenty-one weeks along and almost certainly will not survive at this point. Three: you can let gravity work for you. In that case we'd put you on complete bed rest here in the hospital and position you with your feet raised above your head. You'll remain in that position throughout the duration of your pregnancy, the longer the better. We'll try to buy enough time to enable your baby to mature sufficiently to survive."*

*He stops, looks at us, and asks straightforwardly, "Whaddya think?"*

*I think I want to retch. I think I want God to whisper in my ear what we should do. I think I'd like to push a rewind button so we can* replay the past few days and perhaps intervene before Samuel's situation becomes so dire.

Instead, I turn to Krista and ask lamely, "Honey?"

Abby is spellbound. "Were you scared, Dad?" Was Mom?"

Daniel echoes intently, "You scared, Dad-dee? You scared?"

"Yes, I was," I tell them. "But mommy wasn't. She was just . . . very determined to do everything she could to save Samuel."

*We select option three, hoping that gravity will work some magic for a few weeks, perhaps longer.*

*Krista cedes her hyper-developed sense of independence and desire for control. She stays in bed with her feet lifted slightly above her head for three weeks. No showers, no trips to the bathroom, no social calls to the nurses' station. I become adept at handling a bedpan and Krista becomes skilled at using one. Between this regimen and her frequent pelvic exams, she relinquishes all vestiges of modesty. She adapts remarkably well and is almost always upbeat. She feels good and is confident we've made the right choice in our approach to Samuel's well-being.*

On day twenty-one of Krista's bed rest, another Saturday, I am cutting our lawn when I notice a neighbor running toward me with a terror-stricken expression. I cut the engine just in time to hear her yell that the hospital has been trying to reach me.

"The baby is coming!" she bellows. "Go now!"

I arrive to find Krista bleeding profusely and in agony. Nurses pump magnesium sulfate into her to halt, or at least slow down, the contractions. They administer steroid injections to assist Samuel's last-minute lung development.

Despite best efforts all around, several things go wrong. The contractions cannot be stemmed. Krista endures excruciating pain and severe hemorrhaging due to a placental abruption. Samuel is breach, and thus his trip down the birth canal is a bumpy—even violent—one, and his tiny head is whipped to and fro during delivery. The vulnerable and immature vessels in his brain take a beating and he suffers significant intracranial bleeding. The neonatal intensive care team revives him and whisks him immediately to the NICU, where they apply a plethora of high-tech interventions.

I initially remain with Krista to provide whatever meager comfort I can. After fifteen or twenty *minutes she commands me, "Go see Samuel, Tim. Then come back and tell me everything."*

We're only a couple of miles from Samuel's grave now, and Luke and Daniel are rapt. There are portions of this story they've never heard or have forgotten, so its novelty has cast a spell on them.

Luke asks, "What did he look like, Daddy? What did you do?"

Daniel, our human myna bird, parrots, "What did you do? What did you do?"

*I walk down the hallway and open the door to the outer area of the NICU. We've been given a tour of the facility already, in anticipation of Samuel's likely premature arrival, so I know to wash my hands thoroughly and to put on a sterile gown before entering the inner sanctum.*

*I am faintly aware of others being present, but I focus on the one-pound specimen I immediately know is my son. He is tiny, emaciated, and his skin appears severely sunburned, translucent, fragile, and greasy. His thighs are so tiny my wedding band would fit comfortably around one of them. His limbs are cocked at illogical angles, and his right arm rises and falls slowly but spasmodically. A tube has been inserted down his throat* and it is held in place by adhesive affixed across his mouth. It is connected to a high-frequency ventilator delivering staccato bursts of air to his dysfunctional lungs. His eyes, still fused shut, are covered by gauze to prevent damage from the intense lights that bathe him in ultraviolet rays to ward off jaundice. Beeps and bells create a discordant fugue and signal all manner of medical developments. Blood pressure, oxygen saturation levels, heart rate, and body temperature are under constant surveillance.

I stand next to Samuel, marveling at both my instinctive devotion and his beauty. And then I think, My God. This is how my father feels for me. I had no idea.

Medical personnel constantly minister to Samuel and log his progress. I listen to their pronouncements and mentally file them with as much precision as possible. His condition changes frequently, sometimes by the minute. I spend long stretches next to him atop a tall stool, praying constantly that he can somehow sense he is loved and asking that his fear and pain be alleviated. I talk to him in the most soothing tones I can muster. I gently cup the top of his head with my left hand and the soles of his feet with my right because I yearn to touch him and I want to communicate, somehow, that I'm here and I'm not leaving.

By the third day I feel comfortable changing his diaper, and I exult when he produces waste. The feces he emits resembles, in both size and shape, the lead from a mechanical pencil.

I read to him Green Eggs and Ham and Curious George. I worry, I hover, I plan. I silently ask myself haunting questions: Do you hurt? Do you feel alone? Are you scared? I interact in my inept fashion. After all, he is my son.

In the early morning of the eleventh day, the hospital calls. Someone should come soon, they say.

When I see Samuel, it is clear he is near death. A lung has collapsed, and fluid has filled his chest cavity, placing significant pressure on his heart. A chest tube is protruding from his midsection, and his oxygen saturation levels are pitiful. The brain damage from lack of oxygen is certainly severe by now, and his pallor—there is no way to put this delicately—is grayish, resembling rotten meat. It is time to say goodbye.

Krista, my mother, and I surround Samuel, issuing fervent prayers and weeping. We disconnect the medical machinery, and I hold him in my arms for the first time. We carry him to a *private room and cradle him as tiny bubbles form on his lips as he expires. I cry in heaps, convulsing without control. We hold Samuel and gaze into his handsome face until we come to grips—tenuously—with the reality that he is gone.*

*Two days later my wife, my mother, and I drive twelve hours to Krista's hometown (where we return permanently four years later) with Samuel nestled in his bread-box-sized coffin next to our suitcases. With friends and family at our sides, we bury our newborn son in a pastoral graveyard in a family plot.*

*For a while I am a completely broken man, unable to function beyond the most basic level. In time, though, through a process that is inscrutable and sometimes even imperceptible, I regain my footing for life. I experience laughter again, and feel hope and joy, particularly when three new souls rapidly enter our lives.*

Abby, Daniel, and Luke tumble out of the car, and I lay a blanket next to Samuel's grave.

"What does that say again?" Abby asks, pointing to his headstone.

"It says 'A mighty soul, never forgotten,'" I tell her. It is a line borrowed from the eulogy my father delivered at Samuel's funeral.

"What does that mean?" Abby continues to question.

I smile at each of them, amazed by their personalities, their bodies, their healing qualities, their mere existence. Then I answer.

"I think it means that little Samuel, who never opened his eyes, never took a step, never ate a morsel of solid food, and never uttered a single word, still had a great impact on our sliver of the world. He helped make your arrival and Daniel's and Luke's possible and safe. He helped me to understand how beautiful and special you are and to better appreciate our time together. He helped me to develop patience and faith in the future, even when things seem horrible and confusing. And, like you and your younger brothers, he took me places I never thought I'd go. He taught me how to be a better father."

"Oh," she replies. "Wow."

Luke looks up now, affected by Abby's serious tone of reverence.

So does Daniel, who examines my wistful expression and asks, "You happy, Daddy? You happy?"

"Yes, Daniel," I say truthfully as I pass out the food. "I couldn't be happier."

—*Tim Swensen*

# My Life as a Blankie

My youngest daughter first grabbed a handful of my hair with her chubby little fingers at six weeks of age, and she never really let go. She'd curl up beside me each time her eyelids grew heavy, her honey and walnut locks a puffball against my chest. Then, tiny fingers would snake past my ear, searching for a lifeline. Kayla would twirl my hair with one hand and rub her eyes with the other as she fought her battle against sleep.

Though I adored her and treasured the bond that grew between us, I often longed for my freedom. But *Monday Night Football*, a daddy exhausted from a long day at work, a stack of dirty dishes mocking me from the sink—all failed to gain her sympathy. Kayla never gave up, determined that one night she'd beat that evil slumber and manage to stay awake the rest of her life.

Kayla's third birthday approached. Her cumulative won-lost record against sleep hovered around 0–1,000, and my head felt as threadbare as a one-armed, ready-for-the-landfill teddy bear. I decided to reclaim my evening independence.

Her mother and I set a date a week in advance for Kayla's weaning from her daddy habit. I broke the news as she lay curled beside me. A look of dread crept across her face. Still, she agreed that none of her friends used *their* fathers as sleep aids. She also longed for that honorable "big girl" label. The date of my emancipation finally arrived, and I held her hand as we climbed the steps to her bedroom. Kayla's head sagged low as she made her ascent—a tiny prisoner on her way to the gallows.

My wife and I tucked her in, then turned out all the lights except for Big Bird, smiling from a nearby outlet. Kayla fought against tears her heart wanted to shed but her pride wouldn't allow.

"Good night, Mommy. Night, Daddy. Love you."

Fear glistened in those small, beautiful eyes. They begged for a reprieve, but I refused the last-minute pardon. From the bottom of the stairs, I heard her crying into her pillow. I forced myself to listen as my youngest child fought to break a habit that I should have prevented years before. Although the list of mistakes I've made as a parent is long and impressive, this one had caused one of my children real heartache. I would have whipped myself if I'd owned a switch.

It took almost an hour, but she finally drifted off. I prayed that only wonderful dreams awaited her on the other side.

Unfortunately, when she woke the next morning, it became apparent she'd just traded her sleep problems for another issue.

"D-d-d-d-addy!" she stuttered.

"Good morning, sweetheart." I kissed her and gave her a big hug. "Sleep well?"

"Y-y-yes. Are c-c-car-cartoons on yet?"

I eyed her quizzically. She never stuttered. "Sure are. In fact, it's time for your favorite."

"P-p-p-power Rangers!" she squealed.

In the coming days, the stuttering grew worse. We visited her pediatrician.

"It just started one day?" he asked.

"Yes. She'd never stuttered before, then she woke up one day and started. I thought you should see her."

He had Kayla giggling as he checked her out—not a difficult trick with a child who had trouble taking off her socks without tickling her own feet.

"Any big changes in her life before she started stuttering?" the doctor asked.

"Well, we are trying to get her to fall asleep by herself instead of next to me," I offered. "That's silly, though, I'm sure. Can't be it."

"Can," the doctor said. "I've seen it before when kids try to give up a security blanket or a favorite stuffed animal. She a daddy's girl?"

"Yeah, kinda," I admitted.

"Kinda?" my wife asked, then burst out laughing.

"What should we do, doctor?" I pleaded.

"Well, either let her resume sleeping with you for a couple months before trying again or let her grow up with a stutter. She'll probably outgrow it, but you never know."

"What would you do?"

He paused and studied his patients, both father and daughter. Then he smiled. "Let her sleep with you again, Dad. Although I'm sure it's a bit of an inconvenience, there's really nothing wrong with it. In some cultures, entire families sleep together in one big room. Some studies even suggest it's good for a child. It's just where she feels safe. You're her security blanket."

That night, Kayla fell asleep on the couch while playing with my hair. The next morning, she woke with only a minor stutter and even that disappeared within another day or two.

We decided Kayla would let us know when she

was ready to sleep on her own, and we resumed our routine. In the months that followed, I still craved my freedom, but knowing the depth of my daughter's love comforted me. Her snuggling addiction required a daddy fix, and the honor of receiving that love outweighed any cramping of my lifestyle.

Within six months, Kayla decided to try again, this time with complete success. My evenings were my own again, though there didn't seem to be as much to do as I'd always believed. She still fell asleep next to me once in awhile, but she'd always wake up and stagger up the stairs to sleep in her own room. The crisis faded into memory.

Years later, when Kayla was eleven, I answered the telephone to find a young boy on the other end.

"Is Kayla there?"

I called my daughter and stood just outside the doorway eavesdropping like any competent daddy. The conversation seemed composed mostly of giggling.

Several weeks went by. Valentine's Day arrived, and my daughter's class celebrated by passing out those cheap valentines we all loved as kids.

"How did school go, sweetheart?" I asked after picking her up from daycare.

"Derrick kissed me."

"Say what?"

"Derrick kissed me. He gave me a valentine, then kissed me on the cheek in front of the whole class. Ms. Thomas said, 'Looks like Kayla has a valentine!'"

"Is he nice?"

"Yeah, and he's hilarious. He reminds me of you."

Laugh or cry? I searched my pockets for a coin to flip.

After dinner, Kayla relayed the kissing incident to my wife, who found it adorable. Myself, I just felt the world spinning out of control. This was still my baby girl, after all, and way too young for this "boy" stuff.

I noticed my daughter's eyelids sagging about an hour before her bedtime, and I caved in like a three-dollar lounge chair.

"Kayla, you look tired," I said, patting the spot beside me on the couch. "You can snuggle up with me until bedtime if you'd like."

"And play with hair?" she asked, giggling.

"Yes, dear—until you graduate from college, if you don't mind."

Some days, it's difficult to determine which of us is the security blanket.

—Ed Nickum

# Let's Stop Here, Dad

Karen bought our ten-year-old son, Nick, brand new hiking boots for our trip to Yosemite. He was really excited about them (and the trip). Now, there must be a thousand makes and styles of hiking boots. Mine have taken me to some of the most beautiful spots on the planet. They're beaten up and frayed and fit like a second skin. The boots are size nine Nevados, light-brown suede with forest-green trim. I thought it was funny, then, when I opened the box in Nick's room and pulled out a pair of size five Nevados, light-brown suede with forest-green trim.

Karen had no idea she'd gotten Nick my boots. We were all entertained by the coincidence. Nick was blown away.

"I can't believe we got the same ones, Dad." He looked down at his, looked at mine, kicked dirt on his to get the new sparkle off, to get that worn-in look like mine. "This is so cool, Dad. They're like identical!"

It was in those matching Nevado nines and fives that we set out on our expedition to Yosemite Falls.

Nick's been my walking buddy since, well, since he could walk. One of my favorite pictures of us was taken in Grass Valley, in the gold country of Northern California. He's about five, and we're hiking through the redwoods. Actually, he's on my shoulders, pooped out, our backs to the camera, as the late afternoon sun shoots perfect beams into the forest like a flashlight aimed through a colander.

Now, the guidebook calls the loop to Yosemite Falls an all-day, "strenuous" hike. It's about five miles round trip, nearly a thousand feet up via a series of tight switchbacks and rock ledges to some of the most awe-inspiring vistas you can imagine: the Yosemite Valley sprawled below, majestic Half Dome looming ahead, and our faces so close to the falls we'd be covered in mist. There would be no "pooped" shoulder rides home.

We filled our backpacks with granola bars, a few precious oranges, water, sunscreen. But for Nick, the real preparation was scuffing his boots and grinding enough dirt in to get them to look like he's had 'em as long as I've had mine. He got close.

The first leg of the journey was pretty easy: a shuttle bus ride to the trail head. We sat with our backpacks on our laps and our walking sticks at our sides. From time to time I'd look down at the floor at our four matching hiking boots. I'd look over at Nick, who was sneaking a peek too—and smiling.

The trail begins in woods so thick it's almost dark. A narrow path with intricate rock walls on either side leads the way up. And up and up. Nick practically bounded ahead of me, the concept of pace eluding him. I'd watch him go, like a rabbit in new boots, this strong, exuberant kid just celebrating with every step. My whole body was smiling and proud. And just a little out of breath.

An hour or so into the hike, we broke out of the dappled darkness and found ourselves clinging to the side of a mountain. Well, not clinging, but on a trail so thin and steep that if Karen had seen it she would not have been pleased. The Yosemite Valley rolled out beneath us, and the sound of the falls could be heard off in the distance, like the crowd at Yankee Stadium in a constant home-run cheer.

People who'd already been to the falls passed us on their way back. We'd ask, "How long?" and they'd reply, "'Bout an hour, but it's worth it!" They seemed to us like astronauts who'd been to Mars. Their smiles were our inspiration.

Water seeps down the rock face in trickles. It's as though it can't wait to pour out of the top, so it squeezes its way out wherever possible. We splashed through little puddles and ankle-deep bowls. We walked through stretches of searing gravel, baking in the sun, and moist loamy soil, perpetually damp under the shade of hundred-year-old pines. We walked over solid stone floors, some as hot as skillets, some slick and cool from the run-off.

And we talked. We talked about dinosaurs, and baseball, and dinner. We talked about family, and we talked about grown-ups. We talked about girls and how they can drive guys crazy in so many ways.

And sometimes we just walked.

We listened to the sound of our footfalls on pebbles, on leaves, on twigs. We listened to the mountain bluebirds, and the falls getting closer, and the wind as it swept across the cold face of the mountain and chilled the sweat on our necks.

With every new turn in the trail, we wondered about hikers who'd been here before. These trees sure had seen a lot of people amble by. We ran our hands up the twisted bark and guessed how long the trees had been there. How long would they remain? A hundred years? A million?

We pressed on, saying "hi" to every hiker who passed us on their return trip. The man from Denmark. The couple from France. The Japanese family. The lady whose country we couldn't identify because of her funny accent; we settled on Tonsilvania. They were all different but all the same. All drenched from their journey to the falls, all smiling, all feeling the same thing we'd soon feel.

When you approach a waterfall as powerful as Yosemite, the ground starts doing something weird. There's a hum that comes up through the mountain and goes right into your boots. We knew we were getting closer. The buzz in our feet grew to a rumble, and the Yankee fans were getting louder and louder.

Nick asked me about some of the other hikes I'd been on. I told him about Acadia National Park in Maine and the twenty-two-mile canoe trip on a lake where I never saw a ripple. I told him about the Everglades where I had to wait for the alligator with the diamond eyes to cross the road and the Rockies where I'd hiked in shorts, in August, to the snow. I told him about Ecuador, the time I flew from sea level, up, up, up through the clouds, landing in Quito, and then watched as the plane flew back down through the clouds. I hiked the Andes alongside llamas and alpacas. Mt. Snowden in Wales. Bryce Canyon, Wyoming. Big Sur, California. The Blue Ridge Mountains. Sedona, Arizona.

I gave him details from every journey—smells, sounds, animals, plants, blisters, sprains, sunsets, icy plunges in mountain pools, dizzying, dazzling views from granite balconies. He asked me how I could remember so much. I told him every hike was like a movie I could play whenever I wanted. He said he was making a movie of this hike.

As we spoke, I realized our voices were getting louder and louder. We rounded a corner, and there it was. And it took our breath away. Water just exploding out of the top of this mountain with so much force you think the rock walls can't hold it back. That at any moment, the sculpted, massive stone will just crumble, and an entire lake will fly out in one wet slab. The cascade creates rainbows so thick with color you can practically climb them. And the spray is ice cold and delicious—energizing and narcotic at the same time.

We just stood there for a moment, watching, listening, hearts pounding, feet humming. I was transfixed by the falls, and then glanced over at Nick, transfixed himself. I was looking at two natural wonders: the falls and my little boy's face illuminated by beauty, respect, and awe. I wanted to ask him what he thought, but then I realized I knew.

He wasn't thinking. He was filling up his soul. Just being . . . making his movie. I've never seen him look at anything quite that way. I kept silent, wondering how long this moment would last.

The late afternoon sun bounced off some eternally soaked angle of stone and produced a gold I had never seen before. The color seemed to come from somewhere deep inside the earth, filtered and amplified by minerals and gasses and oils, heated by the molten history of the ages. This golden sparkle hit my eye, breaking the spell. The sun was going down, and it was time to start back.

We passed a few late-comers on their way to the falls. "How much further?" they asked. "About an hour," Nick replied, beaming. "But it's worth it." We'd been to Mars. We were reporting back.

We hiked in silence for a long time. I asked Nick if he wanted a rest, but he said he'd rather keep going. I knew he was tired, but he wouldn't let on. I had no problem letting on. I was ready for a beer and a foot rub.

Just before we entered the last set of switchbacks, that maze of rock-walled paths through thick woods, Nick said, "Let's stop here, Dad."

"Yeah, buddy, let's stop here," I said.

We sat down under the tree that would be our gateway to the last leg of this journey. I leaned against the trunk, my feet throbbing inside my tired boots. Nick sat inside my legs, using my chest as a back rest. He knocked his hiking boots against mine occasionally, just a tap here and there. We opened a backpack, found the last orange, and tore into it.

We were looking at the Yosemite Valley, mesmerized. It was fiery in that fading golden light. The river was a platinum necklace, strewn carelessly across the valley floor. The clouds over Half Dome were roiling, the wisps along their bottoms orangey pink and their ominous ceilings draining from blue to black into the night. And the falls—though we could no longer see it, we could still hear it cheering in the distance. Or was the sound just lingering inside us?

Under that tree, we sat in blissful exhaustion. I felt the weight of Nick's head against my chest, warm over my heart. My mind was swirling with a thousand thoughts. And then one thought rose above the others and became as clear as a single droplet of water: When Nick said, "Let's stop here, Dad" he meant, "Let's stop here for an orange and a granola bar." When I said, "Yeah, buddy, let's stop here," I meant, "Let's stop here forever."

—Judd Pillot

*This essay was first published on FreshYarn.com, 10th Installment, September 15, 2004.*

# Guys Just Want
# to Have Fun

With my family, it takes many retellings of the same story to get to the truth. I often have to surgically probe, expertly wielding my scalpel, to get the facts. Sometimes, I need a shovel; other times, I head straight for the hydraulic excavator. It's part of my reality. It's what helps me get through the day. It makes the voices in my head stop chanting mantra.

Steve, my younger son, was at the age where he wanted to do things alone with his dad. He wanted it to be just the two of them. Dad had become the hero. Dad was Mr. Man. So, when Steve said he wanted to go to the annual family karate camp sponsored by his karate school, I was not surprised that he wanted Sam, my husband, to take him. I had done it the year before, and my memory of it was vastly different from Steve's memory.

I remember it rained the whole weekend. It was extremely cold, and we were dressed for spring. We were assigned to the bunks as families, and ours was the farthest from the outhouses. The outhouses smelled. In the middle of the night, with wild animals ready to pounce on unsuspecting maternal figures, I had to go, all by myself, to this outhouse, because I, of weak bladder, couldn't make it through the night without having to go three or four times. I got a flat tire on the way home.

Steve remembered the weekend as, "Mom never stopped complaining for a minute."

A year later, Sam got his turn. His weekend was dry and warm. The guys were assigned to a bunk right next to the new bathroom facilities. One of the parents who was there was a professional chef, and he volunteered to do all the cooking. Sam said his specialty was French desserts!

About a month later, the truth came out.

"What kind of truck did we get the lift in when we got lost, Dad?" Steve asked Sam. He immediately put his hand to his mouth and turned to leave the room.

"Got lost?" I asked.

Sam continued to play with the remote control, making believe he had a sudden hearing problem.

"Got lost?" I repeated, blocking Steve from making his speedy exit.

Sam, Mr. Cool, Mr. Dad is Great, just left his little buddy to sink by himself. There was no way out, so Sam knew it was a waste to tread water.

Nevertheless, Steve did not know this as he paddled his way solo through the rough waters of Mom's Twenty Questions.

"Well, Dad said it was okay."

"What was okay?" I asked.

Sam sat there staring at the TV with small beads of sweat on his forehead. I was now blocking Sam's view of the TV with my body.

"Um . . . well . . . Dad said I didn't have to go to the karate classes, so we went on a hike."

"You went to karate camp but didn't do any karate?" Sam moved his head to the left to watch the end of the Chuck Norris movie. I blocked him with a shift of my hips.

"We had fun, Mom. We went down a road, and we saw a beaver, a lake, and an old abandoned car, and we ate berries."

"Berries?" I had visions of Hansel and Gretel.

"Yeah. We didn't realize how far we had walked, and it got real hot, and we forgot water, and we left the cell phone in the car. Then Dad didn't know where to go, so we kept walking, and then we finally got to a road. Then Dad said we should go down the road, and it was a big hill, so we did. When we got to the bottom, we saw a sign, and then Dad said he thought we might be going in the wrong direction. So we went back up the hill. We were really thirsty then. We sat on the side of road, but no cars came for a long time. Then finally a real cool truck came and drove us back to camp."

"Drove you back to camp?"

"It had a real cool gun rack in the back."

This past summer, Sam decided to go fishing.

"You know that guy Rocky, the guy at work who's really into camping? Well, he found this great place to fish and gave me a map. I was thinking we should go."

"I'm not going," I said.

"Just you and me, Adventure Boy," Sam said to Steve.

It suddenly occurred to me that "we" never did include me.

"Sam, have you ever gone fishing?" I asked.

His lack of an answer reminded me of a cool truck with a gun rack. For the next few weeks, Sam and Steve prepared lists and made plans. They discussed the food they would cook. They bought a tent. They bought outdoor cooking and eating utensils. They bought candles and flashlights.

Then they started.

I'd be walking through the house and I'd hear Sam say, "And what do you do if you see a grizzly bear?"

"Stop, drop, and roll, Dad?"

"No, that's if you catch fire from the campfire," Sam would say as they both giggled.

They'd wait for my reaction. I didn't disappoint.

Then Adventure Dad and Adventure Boy would laugh and say, "You're such a mom."

The day of the fishing expedition arrived. The men went and did their camping thing. They returned two days later with grand tales of the shark that got away and the bear they scared by singing sitcom theme songs in two-part harmony.

However, the true adventure could not be kept a secret very long. The details began to emerge the moment they started unloading the Jeep upon their arrival home.

"Look, Mom. It was so hot the candles melted. We never even lit them."

From the family room of our air-conditioned home, I'd heard on the news that it had been 115 degrees in Phoenix that day. It never occurred to me that their "cool" fishing spot was only a half-hour away rather than a cooler place up in the mountains and out of the dangerous summer heat of the Arizona desert.

I overheard Sam tell Steve, "Next time, we have to bring a lot more water."

Then, one night, I was sitting in my family

room, relaxing in the relative calm of an ordinary day. Life was smooth and nothing could upset my equilibrium . . . until I saw the cat backing away from something crawling on the rug. We live in Arizona, so occasionally large arachnids and their distant cousins like to come into our home to get out of the heat.

Steve noticed what was going on, and said, "Hey, Dad, is that as big as the scorpion that bit me when we went fishing?" He immediately put his hand to his mouth and turned to leave the room.

"He got bit by a scorpion?" I asked Sam.

"It was a small one," Steve said. "And it didn't really hurt that bad. Not after about two hours."

"He got bit by a scorpion?"

"Really, Mom. Don't get mad at Dad. It was my fault. I didn't shake out my sneakers before I put them back on after they dried after I fell in the lake."

"You fell in the lake?"

"Well, not fell, exactly. I got scared of the snake, and I was backing up from it, and I kind of wound up in the lake."

"Snake?"

"A small snake, Mom. Not as big as the one we saw later that night."

"Two snakes?"

"That's why we slept in the Jeep, Mom."

"You slept in the Jeep?"

"Well, we didn't actually sleep, Mom. It was really hot."

"Even with the top off?"

"We put it back up, Mom, and we zipped up the windows."

"I'm afraid to ask."

"Bats, Mom. Thousands of bats."

"Bats?"

"At least it wasn't a mountain lion, Mom!" Steve was teasing me now, a carbon copy of Sam. "You were right about how she'd react, Dad. She's such a . . ."

I finished the sentence, "I know, I'm such a Mom." A few hours later, Sam and I were sitting together on the couch watching a movie I'd rented. It was one of those chick flicks that I make Sam suffer through occasionally to remind him that I am sailing solo in a sea of men.

"Why didn't you just leave everything and come home if it was so unsafe?" I asked.

Sam gave me the perfect answer. "Because we were having so much fun."

—*Felice Prager*

*A version of this story was first published under the title "It Takes a Mom to Discover the Real Story" in the* Christian Science Monitor, *August 2, 2006.*

# Ain't No Tornado
# Strong Enough

The April morning dawned innocently enough. We all went our separate ways: Cathy and I to elementary school, Dad to his job at the Ohio Air National Guard (OANG) base in Springfield, while Mom held down the fort at home.

I was five years old. Today was Papaw's birthday, and I was looking forward to my own birthday at the end of the month and to Easter in just ten days. Although I loved school, I anticipated great times catching worms, playing baseball, and visiting my grandparents down on the Ohio River that summer.

After school, I huffed along to keep up with Cathy's long strides. She never once looked behind to make sure I was progressing, so I had to put the wheels on or be left behind. She walked even faster on the way home than she did on the way to school, but I didn't care. Without a time limit, I lollygagged more than ever, even stooping to pick a few grape hyacinths that grew by the driveway.

As soon as we got into the house, Mom turned us around and piled us into the Maverick for a quick trip to Rinks to return some faulty merchandise. It was 3:45 P.M.

It began to rain and thunder as we pulled away from the Rinks parking lot, headed for home. Mom said it must be a spring shower. We noticed how the lightning seemed to hang longer than usual in the sky.

The three of us watched the developing storm from Mom and Dad's bedroom once we got home. We noticed that all the birds had suddenly flown away and the sky looked an eerie green.

"Don't worry, girls. Lightning can't hurt you as long as it stays outside."

In Springfield, twenty-five miles away, a storm was pelting the OANG base with golf ball–sized hailstones. My uncle, who also worked at the base, went out with some other men to collect the odd projectiles in buckets. They all looked toward Xenia, our hometown, at the darkening sky. It was 4:30 P.M.

The conversations around him began to sink into Dad's consciousness. The buzz throughout the base repeated that a severe storm, a tornado, had hit Xenia. The city was heavily damaged; people were dead . . .

He grabbed the nearest phone and dialed home. Nothing. He dialed zero.

"Operator."

"I'm trying to call 513-372-1372, and I get nothing."

"What city?"

"Xenia. I'm calling my wife in Xenia."

"Oh, sir, don't you know? Xenia's been destroyed."

"What do you mean, destroyed? My wife and kids are there!"

"Sir, no one can get in or out of Xenia."

The dangling phone bounced once, twice, went dead.

Dad stopped to tell Uncle Wayne, "I'm leaving. I'm going to Xenia."

"Wait! I'll go with you!" Wayne called out, then stopped.

Dad was already running, with heavy black boots and a heavier heart, to his car, to home. He did not drive the speed limit.

Suddenly, traffic came to a halt. Vehicles were lined up under a gray sky along Route 68 South for miles, all the way to Detroit Street. His eyes were already searching for his wife and children. His heart was pounding at the lack of action, his brain screaming at him to *Go! Go! Go! Now! Now! Now!*

He abandoned the vehicle and started to run, galvanized by the hammer in his chest. He ran down North Detroit, pacing himself, beginning to get into a rhythm now that he'd broken away from the gridlock of traffic and mounting hazards of debris.

He slowed as he caught sight of the bike shop ahead on the right. Ever a moral man, he swore to himself that, no matter what happened, he would return the bike he now commandeered. His heart melted within him from fear as he half rode, half jogged through town with the handlebars firmly in his grip. The big stately homes in town were nothing but piles of wood, glass, bricks, and personal belongings of the occupants. Trees that had stood since Xenia's founding now lay across streets, cars, and houses. Sirens blasted everywhere, and rain was beginning to fall.

He got to the center of town and turned right on Route 35. The train that next blocked his path had apparently been thrown like a two-year-old's toy across the city's heart. Without a second thought, he rode straight for the closest boxcar, catapulted from the bike, and scrabbled underneath, dragging the bike behind. Adrenalin kept him going. No thought was spared for shifting tons of metal or the pain of knees and shoulders on tracks of rail and gravel or the burden of the bike. His heart strained to the point of explosion.

Once free of the train, he hopped on the bike again and continued on. People were gathered at the nearby A&W Root Beer stand, mourning the dead and dying. Nothing could stop him until he knew about Lois and the girls. The love of his life had been a girl of twenty when she'd met the loneliest soldier on leave from the Army in 1963 and married him in '64. For her, he'd made his leave permanent. In 1965, they welcomed their baby daughter Cathy, now an independent, scrawny nine-year-old and the apple of his eye. Lainie, bright-eyed and worshipful of her big sister, was a Xenian by right of her birth in 1968.

*Had the girls been in school, away from both Mommy and Daddy . . . ? Oh, my God,* he prayed. *Let them be safe.*

Kroehler Furniture looked as though it had exploded. Semi trailers were tossed like toy blocks. The store was only a few miles from home—the *home*, not house, he'd built with Lois. He'd promised to love and protect them all—and now this, while he was at work.

He rode faster in spite of the upward slant of the road that heaved his lungs. *Please, God. Please.*

He turned into the Arrowhead subdivision and raced past people out in their trashed yards, crying, screaming, or calling someone's name. For the first time, he thought of neighbors. The unknown could not be borne; he put everything out of his mind except his destination. He looked at Maumee Drive and became disoriented. Which way was home? So many houses were gone, and everyone's walls, roofs, and furniture were mixed together in the yards and streets.

He almost slammed into a brown van turned upside down in the middle of the street as he careened onto Pueblo Drive. He knew he was on the right street, but where was home? Where was Lois? How could she possibly be here? When he'd left that lovely spring morning, he'd driven past neat rows of houses and lawns. Now, there was nothing but rubble.

Out of the blue, he remembered: *Today is Carl's birthday. He's seventy and his daughter is dead, and I wasn't here.*

Starting at the corner, he counted houses until he found his own. The Osborne's house on the left was gone; only the slab remained. On the other side, the Turner's house consisted of two bathroom walls standing among the bricks, shingles, glass, and garbage; the family was on vacation.

*This is our house. At least it's still here. Maybe . . . maybe they made it!* He was afraid to think, to hope.

"Lois!" A pause. "Lois!"

The living room was a cataclysm of glass and

two-by-fours. He could see the sky through gaping holes in the roof. Two boiled eggs sat on the kitchen stove in a pot of water. The stove clock was frozen at 4:40 P.M.

*Then, they weren't in school . . . Where are they?*

"LOIS!" he cried with all his being.

He turned, and she was there. They cried and clung together as if driven through one another's heart by the tornado itself. Suddenly, he thrust her to arms' length.

"The girls. Where—?"

"They're at the Sewells'."

Doris Sewells' house, two doors down, was fairly intact.

Together, they ran to their daughters.

Cathy, shocked and silent, allowed his hug to swallow her.

"Daddy?" I tugged at his pants leg.

"Yes, baby." He knelt.

"Will the Easter Bunny be able to find me here if I'm not at home?"

"The Easter Bunny is just like Daddy, honey." He looked over my head with a weary smile at Mommy. "He can find you anywhere."

—Elaine Williams

# Heirlooms

My infant son, Damon, yawns delicately. Wrapped in a blue blanket that frames his pink face, he works his left arm free.

I reach into the bassinet and lovingly place the little finger of my left hand, the hand closest to my heart, into my baby's hand.

In response, Damon makes infant noises and wraps his whole hand around my finger.

Proud Papa here is delighted. I smile at him with tears in my eyes.

"You will hold my hand for a little while, my son," I tell him. "But you'll hold my heart forever."

"Pirates of the Caribbean or Small World?" I ask Damon.

His fingers squeeze the duck bill on the front of his hat. *Quack!*

He looks up with his pretty blue eyes and finds me laughing and asking, "Is that a 'no' quack or a 'yes' quack?"

His little fingers reach for the duck bill again. *Quack, quack!*

He is three years old, and even though we don't speak the same language, we travel well together.

I take his left hand and we go see Pirates of the Caribbean. Damon quacks his approval.


"How come your mom fed you tomatoes all the time?" Damon asks.

He's watering our egg-size heirlooms in our back-yard garden.

I smile at him and say, "My father didn't work every day, like I do, so we often didn't have money to buy food. Our garden gave us lots of vegetables, not just tomatoes.

"Then my dad died, and we really needed our garden."

My son is six years old and curious about family history.

"Do you miss your dad?" he asks.

His question causes my weed-pulling to stop and me to ponder: *Do I miss my dad? Hmmm.*

I look at Damon and his curly hair in the bright sunshine and enjoy where I am.

"Some people you remember," I say. "Some people you miss. I remember my father."

"Look at that one, Dad! Wow!"

Damon points out yet another falling star.

I keep our tent open and allow the night sky, salted with stars, to entertain my son during our camp out. He falls asleep with his left arm extended. I take his ten-year-old hand in mine and hold on as I make a wish upon a falling star:

*Could I please watch my son grow through adulthood?*

"Dad, when are you coming home?" Damon says over Friday night pizza.

"I thought you understood—" I start to say.

Then I realize there is no right language for communicating divorce to a twelve-year-old. My attempt to protect my son from feelings of abandonment has failed and I feel awful.

"I'm sorry," I say.

I reach for his hand. He pulls away.

Those drugs he took still terrify me.

Being called to the warehouse and having his boss tell me to go in the backroom and get my son reminds me of times my mother sent me into Huesner's smelly bar to get my dad. I disliked having to tell my dad to stop drinking and come home.

Forty years after I led my father out of a dark saloon, I lead my son out of a dark warehouse.

I lost my dad early. I don't want to lose my son at all.

Damon stands silently on my front porch. His green sleeping bag, his bass guitar, his coin collection box, his Charlie McCarthy puppet—all of his possessions are beside him. Damon is sixteen years old and has left his mother's house to live with me.

I slowly open the front door, reach out, and solemnly take his hand in mine. I speak into his blue eyes and say, "I never left you, son."

"You have a granddaughter!" Damon shouts to me over the telephone. He's in his second year of junior college and Life has stomped on his fast-forward button.

After he graduates, he moves his family back to Ohio State for his bachelor's degree, followed by his master's degree, followed by a job opportunity in Germany.

When I complain about him leaving for Europe with his wife pregnant, my son explains to me, "Dad, people in Germany have babies all the time."

"I bought a round-trip ticket," Damon says when I pick him up at the airport.

His family has stayed in Europe while he's come home to San Francisco to attend a clinic specializing in treating people who suffer from depression.

We drive home slowly. He tells me the birth of his son went well. His daughter is learning German easily.

His blue eyes are dark-looking and scary. I don't like how he's talking and am fearful of the dark feelings that he projects.

"Major clinical depressive disorder" is the diagnosis. Damon checks himself into a nearby clinic as an outpatient.

Three months later, experts pronounce him healthy. He happily waves his graduation diploma in my warm kitchen as he telephones the airlines. All he talks about is how he misses his children.

Being served with divorce papers sets off a depressive episode. He cancels his flight.

When his children move with their mother to Florida, Damon moves to a confused state of mind for a few years. He accepts state disability. He sells his coin collection and his bass guitar. I hide his Charlie McCarthy puppet.

The only time Damon lifts his head is when I say, "I care about you, son."

The blueness gradually emerges in his eyes. He works his way off medication and eats only organics.

"Will you help me with my children next summer?" Damon asks. He stops picking vegetables, stands up, smiles, and says, proudly, "I'll be working every day."

Before twilight falls, I am barely able to finish watering Damon's garden. He takes pride in his work. His garden is weed-free. I note his beans, corn, and a long straight row of heirloom tomato plants.

Damon is carrying a bag of fresh vegetables from his garden when he stops and says, "I love you, Dad." He bites into a ripe tomato and goes into his house.

My tears are salty or I'd water the garden with them. Instead, I stand holding the hose and looking at all we have created together. My thirty-five-year-old son has his health, his career, his own place, and he's eating right. I feel blessed.

Heirlooms: you nurture them and care for them, and they grow into something beautiful and productive. The best ones are homegrown with loving hands.

—*John J. Lesjack*

# The Amazing Powers
# of Super–Hero Dad

As the only female (read, voice of sanity) and the stay-at-home parent (read, domestic CEO) in our home, my family accepts that I embody several Justice League powers that my guys can only read about in comic books. My X-ray vision can see past the jar of mayonnaise in the refrigerator to find the pickle jar. My finely tuned sense of smell can locate a dirty sock from the opposite end of the house. And my saliva is both an anesthetic and an antiseptic. Yes, I am a Super Heroine the likes of which neither Marvel nor DC comics has yet to immortalize. I am marvelous. I can do anything. Well . . . almost anything. Let's face it, even Superman can't withstand Kryptonite. And, as I learned a few years ago, my Kryptonite comes in the form of a tiny, white bit of calcium—the baby tooth.

"Mommy, look at this!" announced my son J.P., sticking his finger in his mouth and wiggling his tooth ever so slightly.

"How nice," I choked as I averted my gaze from his mouth. "It's your first loose tooth."

"When will it come out?"

I felt a strange churn in my stomach. "I don't know. That's a good question for Daddy."

I turned tail and flew into the bathroom, swiftly locking the door behind me so as not to be followed in by my still-excited son. I splashed cold water on my face, sat on the edge of the bathtub, and reverted back to Lamaze breathing to gain control of my body. I have always had an issue with teeth. Oh sure, they're fine when they line up straight in a person's mouth. And they're quite useful for eating. But when they wiggle and fall out, my brain turns fuzzy, my knees convert to Jell-O, and I dissolve into a puddle of quivering slime. Okay, so maybe that's a slight exaggeration, but the point remains: I prefer teeth *in* the mouth, not out of the mouth. I didn't enjoy the process of losing teeth when I was a kid, and I certainly wasn't ready to change my mind anytime soon.

Enter *my* Super Hero, my husband and the father of our children, Jean-Marc. Upon arriving home from work and being pounced upon by J.P., Jean-Marc suddenly transformed from retail manager to

Super Dad. Super Dad did not squirm at the sight of the wobbly fang. Super Dad thought it was super cool. He taught J.P. how to keep his mouth closed and wiggle his tooth with his tongue so that "the color will return to Mommy's pale face."

For the weeks that followed, Super Dad kept tabs on the tooth's progress, accurately predicted the day it would come out, and when it did fall out, helped our son rinse his mouth. Super Dad even held the little dagger in the palm of his hand without getting nauseous or fainting, boldly sealing it safely into a Ziploc plastic storage bag.

That night, with the tooth safely sealed in its air-tight isolation chamber and tucked under J.P.'s pillow, I felt strong again. So confident was I that my full super powers had returned that I joyfully awaited the sound of my son's snoring so I could morph into the Tooth Fairy for the first time. Unfortunately, snack-bag plastic does not shield this Superwoman from her Kryptonite.

"What are you doing in my room, Mommy?" J.P. asked, springing up from his bed.

Immediately, I jumped into offensive mode. "What are you doing up?"

"I heard you come into my room."

My light sleeper's use of logic required a change of tactic on my part. "Did you call for me?"

"No."

"Oh. I thought for sure I heard you call out my name."

"You must be hearing things."

"I must be. Okay, then, well, as long as you're okay," I said tucking him in extra tightly and kissing his forehead. "Go back to bed."

"Mom?"

"Yes?"

"Did the Tooth Fairy come yet?"

*She's trying, kid!*

"Not yet, honey. Go back to bed so she can, okay?"

"Okay."

I skulked back to my bedroom.

"How'd it go?" asked my husband.

"Not so good. But it's early still. I'll try again later."

Later went just as badly. My excuse for being in his room the second time was that I thought his room smelled muggy and I needed to open his window.

During my third try, I explained to my son that it was getting too cold and I was in his room to close his window.

Dejected, I flopped into bed, waking my husband in the process.

"What time is it?" he asked.

"Three o'clock."

"What are you doing up?"

*Failing as a mother.*

I proceeded to share my Tooth Fairy failures with him.

"It's impossible," I concluded. "The kid is such a light sleeper that there's no way to sneak in there, get the tooth from under his pillow, and replace it with the money. I never liked this whole tooth thing and now I like it even less."

My husband kissed my pouting lips. "Where's the money?"

"Here." I dropped the quarters into his hand; their ringing echoed my death toll as a Super Heroine. I pulled the covers over my head as I heard my husband open our bedroom door.

Within a matter of minutes, he returned.

"Mission accomplished," he said, snuggling up to me.

I flipped the covers off my head. "What? What do you mean 'mission accomplished?'"

Jean-Marc dangled the tooth-filled Ziploc in front of my face.

"How?"

"Well, when I walked into his room, he immediately sat up and asked me what I was doing in his room. I told him that he needed to go to the bathroom. So, while he was in the john, I switched out the tooth for the money."

Stunned by his simple solution to my humongous problem, all I could think to say was, "You're a devious S.H.D."

"S.H.D.?"

"Super–Hero Dad."

Since that first Tooth Fairy incident, Super Dad has made many more appearances in our home, and we've made some amazing discoveries as a result. Super Dad's saliva has the same anesthetic and antiseptic powers as mine. He's got a bit of X-ray vision where the refrigerator is concerned too. And although his olfactory system is not as acute as mine, Super Dad can withstand a little boy "stink bomb" long enough to retaliate with a "manly" one of his own.

Yes, I am marvelous. I can do just about anything. But the Justice League is definitely more powerful and more fun with the incredible Super Dad in it too.

—*Judy L. Adourian*

# Tough Little
# Dirt Dobber

"Hey, Willy, let's go out to the Harrison lease and play."

When Buddy says that, it means Pat, his pa, won't be around to smack him and say no.

I know what I'm talking about. Buddy's my best friend and he lives across the road from me.

When Pat isn't driving a bulldozer or beating up on Buddy or Buddy's ma, he spends most of his spare time at the Nonesuch Pool Hall playing Moon. The men who work in the oil fields around my hometown of Nonesuch, Texas, hang out at the pool hall. They usually come in straight from work in their greasy overalls, steel-toed boots, and hard hats. The first thing they do after they wrap their calloused hands around a longneck is start playing Moon. All I know about Moon is you play it with dominoes and you always slam them down hard enough to shake the table and you cuss a lot. I don't know if you have to drink beer to play, but everybody does.

Everybody but Daddy. He's always working in the drugstore. He never cusses, smokes, chews, or shoots pool like a real man. He never even goes in a pool hall. The only domino game he knows is that sissy game, Forty-Two. Sometimes I wish he was more like the men in town—tall, strong, and brown from working in the sun. He's so puny and pale-skinned. He wears an apron like a girl—jerking sodas, filling prescriptions, making people laugh at his corny jokes. It's embarrassing.

Daddy brings home a quart of ice cream every night after he closes the store at nine. We sit outside on the back steps to eat it, and I can hear the noise and music from the pool hall. I wonder why Daddy isn't over there playing Moon with the real men.

Buddy's and my favorite place to play is the old Harrison oil lease, a couple of miles from town. The land is white alkali and blow sand. Nothing grows on it but tumbleweeds, cats claw, and greasewood. A lot of old rusty pump jacks and other worn-out oil field machinery sit around, and there's a big cooling tank made out of wooden staves where we swim.

There are six shallow oil wells, called "rod line pumpers." The pump things are run from a central powerhouse. The engine makes a deep rumbling *harrump, harrump, POP! harrump, harrump, POP!* sound as it makes a huge wheel go back and forth. This pushes and pulls the long strings of rods connected to each oil well, and that makes the pump things go up and down.

It's a great place to fool around.

Today, Buddy decides to be a tightrope walker and tries to balance himself on a moving rod line. He catches his big toe in some kind of pulley and traps his toe.

Buddy screams and falls to the ground, his toe stuck.

"Ow, ow, ow! Help me, Willy," he yells.

My bare feet frozen to the hot sand, I simply watch idiotically as the moving rod squashes his toe.

"You've got to stop the rod line so we can get my toe out!" He points to a short post with a hole where the rod goes through. "There's a knockoff post."

I scream, "Yeah, so?"

Blood runs down his foot and drips on the ground.

"There—ugh—there should be a knockoff block lying around there somewhere. Oh, man, hurry up. The knockoff block's—ow!—a short piece of pipe with a slit cut in one side. Slip it on the rod line on the other side of the post between the C–link and the post. Ow! Hurry up, dammit."

I scream, "What's a C–link?"

"It's a C-shaped link, you dumbass! It connects the part of the rod line that's—ooh!—squashing my damned toe and the part of the rod line that comes off—ow!—the damned band wheel."

Tears drip off his nose, making a damp spot in the sand.

"After you set the—ugh!—knockoff block, pull the C–link out of the coupling on each rod end. That'll disconnect the—ooo!—whole thing and stop the rod line so we can get my toe out. Ow! Just do it!"

I run to the thingy-post where he points.

Buddy nods. "Yeah, that's it." He drops his head on his arms, his breath coming in weak gasps.

I try to do what Buddy says. I smash my own finger, but I can't figure out how to stop the damned rod line. He's trapped.

"Run over to the county road and stop somebody— anybody," Buddy says. "Oh God! It hurts. Gimme your pocketknife."

"What for?"

"Just give it to me, stupid."

I hand over the knife and run to the road, hardly feeling the rocks cutting my bare feet. I cry and hold my bleeding finger while I wait for help.

Before long, an oilfield winch truck appears.

The driver is Boomer Bancroft, a friend of Buddy's. In the truck with him are three roustabouts: Boog Bledsoe and Richard and Raymond Ledbetter.

I hold my bloody finger up and babble, "Buddy got his toe caught in the pulley thing and he's bleeding, and I smashed my finger and . . ."

Boomer says, "Get in, Willy. Show me where Buddy is. Raymond, find a clean rag for his finger."

I point, and he guns the engine. Chains, tongs, and wrenches rattle as the truck bounces across the pasture toward the Harrison lease.

Buddy is sprawled, unconscious, several feet from where I left him. He holds my knife in one hand. His toe is still in the . . .

"He cut it off!" I scream.

Richard says, "Go get a drink of water, Willy."

Boomer gently shakes Buddy. "Buddy, you okay?"

Buddy opens his eyes, and Boomer says, calm as all git-out, "Aw, you ain't hurt, you little shit. That's what you two river rats get for fartin' around out here."

In a daze, I watch Boomer walk to the truck. He dips his finger in a big can.

"What's that? I ask.

"Pipe dope," says Raymond.

Boomer pulls out a gob and smears it on Buddy's bloody stump. He removes his undershirt and wraps the whole mess with it.

"Let's go," he says.

"What about his toe?" I say.

Boomer looks at Buddy. "You want it?"

Buddy actually grins and nods his head. I wonder why he would want the yucky thing.

Boomer says, "Booger, set the knockoff block and get his toe out of that doll head. Be sure to put the C–link back."

Buddy shoves the severed toe, covered with blood and sand, in his pocket. He wipes my knife on his pants and hands it to me.

I turn my head away and gag. "Keep it."

Riding back to town, Buddy sits up front with his foot propped up on the dashboard and shoots the bull with Boomer, as unconcerned as if he lost a toe every day.

Raymond asks Buddy, "How the hell could you cut off your own toe like 'at?"

"Aw, it was just hangin' on by a little skin and gristle." I don't remember anything else until we get to town.

Buddy steps slowly out of the truck and says, "Thanks, Boomer. I'll have Mama wash your under-shirt." He limps unaided into the doctor's office.

Richard says, "I didn't know pipe dope had medicinal qualities."

"Me neither," says Boomer.

Booger, who hadn't said a word the entire time, shakes his head and chuckles. "Tough little dirt dobber, ain't he?"

I walk in and watch Doc snip off some skin from the stump and sew it up. He smears it with some black, smelly stuff and bandages it. Buddy doesn't make a peep.

Doc explains, "That's Icthamol ointment, made outta fish. It sucks the pizen out."

Buddy says, "It stinks worse than the pipe dope."

"If it gets to hurtin' tonight, have your ma soak it in kerosene. I'll send your pa the bill."

Buddy looks scared. "Doc, please don't tell Pa. He'll beat up on me again. Can't I work it out?"

"Aw, git outta here. There's no charge."

Doc calls after us. "Don't you kids go near nothing more mechanical than a wheelbarrow after this, y'hear?" Buddy's afraid to go home, so we hide out for awhile. I ask, "How'd you get to know so much about knockoff blocks and C–links and all that oilfield stuff?"

"Boomer taught me. Me and him go way back. I'm gonna be a gang-pusher like him someday."

It's after dark when I walk up the alley to my dad's drugstore. Just as I approach the back door, a huge man jumps from the shadows and grabs me. It's Buddy's pa. He smells like beer. He jerks me off my feet.

"Where's Buddy, you little . . ."

I wet my pants.

I hear Daddy say, "Turn him loose, Pat, or I'll crack your skull."

Pat drops me and turns around. "I'm looking for Buddy."

My dad is about half Pat's size. He stands there in the half-dark, wearing his sissy little white apron and holding a sawed-off pool cue. "Go on home, Pat. And don't be mean to Buddy. Doc told me he got hurt and he needs a little kindness."

Dad walks up to Pat and shakes the pool cue in his face. "Don't come around here anymore until you sober up. And don't you ever touch my boy again."

Later, I look out from the screened-in porch where Granddaddy and me sleep. I can see Buddy's house across the road. All the lights are on, and I hear sounds of fighting. "Don't hit him no more, Pat. Stop it. You'll kill him."

"Shut up, woman. You want some of this, too?"

I'm walking to Sunday school next day when I hear, "Willy, wait up." Buddy's bruised face is scrubbed, he wears a sock over his bandaged foot, and he's grinning from ear to ear.

I can't believe it. "Your pa nearly killed you last night. How can you be so cheerful?"

"Aw, he's gettin' old. He can't hit half as hard as

he used to. Hey, look what I got." He pulls out a snuff can and screws off the lid. "Ta da!"

Inside, black with dried blood, showing crushed bone and rotting flesh, is Buddy's toe.

"Let's go scare some girls!" he smirks.

The image of my puny dad, wearing his sissy little apron and bluffing out the meanest son-of-a-bitch in Nonesuch, Texas, comes to my mind (and will stay with me all my life). *Buddy ain't the only tough little dirt dobber in this town*, I think.

I face Buddy and say, "My dad may wear an apron and he may not play Moon, but he can throw a silver dollar, bounce it off the floor higher'n his head and catch it, and he can balance a half-full Coke glass on an Indian-Head nickel, and he can smell a health inspector coming a mile away, and he tells the funniest jokes and makes the best pimiento-cheese sandwich in the whole wide world, and he's the bravest man in Nonesuch, Texas. He brings home ice cream every night, and me and him eat it on the back steps. And I wanta grow up to be just like him."

—*William M. Barnes*

# Drop the Bike

Dad eased my bike down the three steps and handed it to me. Our house had no garage, so ever since I could remember, we had been lugging our bikes up and down the front steps to our enclosed front porch. While it was always a little scary to carry our bikes down the stairs and some strength was required to put them away, we were happy to have a storage space for bikes and outdoor toys that was protected from the harsh elements of the New England seasons.

"Where are we going?" I asked as I took my bike from Dad and wheeled it toward the driveway. "We'll see," he replied as he disappeared into the depths of the porch for his own ancient black three-speed.

At the beginning of summer, I had graduated from my small red bike to a larger hand-me-down turquoise bike that had belonged to my sister. Now, I had finally grown tall enough to ride it without having to stretch my legs and point my toes to reach the pedals, though it was still undeniably big for me. Of course, that didn't matter one iota to me; I was just happy to go on a ride with my dad.

One of the best things about weekend bike rides with Dad was that he led and we followed. We never knew where we would end up until we got there. Our small college town had plenty of side roads, pathways, and dirt roads, so he would take us on a different adventure each time.

Today, Dad and I were going on a bike ride alone; Mom and my sister were off on a Girl Scout field trip for the day. I was Dad's responsibility, though I liked to think he was mine.

Dad lifted his bike to the sidewalk and locked the front door behind him. He mounted his bike, then looked back at me and asked, "Ready?"

I nodded and stepped on the pedal. The bike started to move, and I slid myself onto the seat.

After taking a warm-up lap around the block, we picked up our speed. My sweater, which I had donned as protection against the still cool temperatures of New England's late spring, blew in the breeze created by my movement. Recent days had been almost summer-like, but today the air held the last vestiges of spring.

Dad led us down the street past the brook where we sometimes caught frogs and by the field where we found our milkweed caterpillars each summer. We pedaled at a leisurely pace as we made our way "downtown." Every now and then, a neighbor or acquaintance would wave from a yard, and Dad would wave back, sometimes including a terse "Hi" or a nod of his head. Every so often, he would look back and check to make sure I was still close enough that he didn't need to alter his pace.

Dad turned onto Main Street, and I followed him through the town's business district, if you could call it that. It consisted of a single street less than a quarter-mile long lined with the post office, a drugstore, the newsstand, a coffee shop, and a few mom-and-pop stores scattered here and there to accommodate the needs of the college students. Because of the congestion on this narrow street, we rode on the sidewalks, careful to pedal around the pedestrians.

Leaving the business district, we returned to the road and traveled through the campus. Dad cut through one of the smaller quads and along a footpath between the buildings. Since it was early June, the college was no longer in session, but there were still some students lingering in town as well as a skeleton staff for the upcoming summer programs.

We pedaled up the road behind the savings bank and around one of the dining halls onto a narrow dirt path that took us to the back of the building.

We arrived at a walkway that led down a steep flight of stairs set into a hill. Dad stopped and got off his bike, and I did the same.

"Are we going to go down the stairs?" I asked, eyeing the angle at which the stairs cut into the hill.

Dad shook his head. "We're going down next to them," he pointed to the dirt slope adjacent to the concrete. "But we're going to walk."

He turned to survey the hill, then looked back at me. "It's too steep to ride."

That, I realized, was my admonishment for next time, when I might end up here by myself.

"It definitely is steep," I agreed, feeling my heart begin to pick up its pace just a bit. I stood at the top of the hill watching Dad walk down the hill nonchalantly, his bike obediently rolling next to him.

Getting up my nerve, I started to walk down the slope, holding my bike at bay and trying to be as nonchalant as Dad. My muscles tensed as the bike's weight tugged at my thin arms, pulling me down the hill. I dug in my heels and stiffened my arms, trying to throw my weight back up the hill to counter the bike's natural tendency to pick up speed as it gave in to gravity and the laws of physics. My face must have shown my fear as I ran down the hill, giving over control to the bike.

At the bottom, I slowed my pace—and that of the bike—coming to rest about two feet from Dad. His face was skewed with a mix of helplessness and amusement at watching my bike drag me at top speed down such a steep hill.

"Next time just drop the bike," he said.

"What?" I straightened from the bent-over position I'd assumed trying to catch my breath and soothe the stitch in my side. "What did you say?"

"Next time just drop the bike. If you'd dropped it, it would have fallen and stopped and you could have walked down the hill. If it's pulling you out of control, let it go."

I looked at him sheepishly and nodded. "Good point." What an obvious solution to a situation I'd created by relinquishing control. What a simple means to accomplish my goal of getting down that hill. "Drop the bike."

I've relied on that piece of fatherly advice many times over the years. Whenever circumstances threaten to spin out of control and pull me down with them, I remember that day, see my dad standing at the bottom of the hill waiting to catch me, and think, *Drop the bike.*

—*Suzanne Schryver*

# Being Daddy

I entered fatherhood through the nontraditional path: I married a woman with two children from a previous marriage. When I officially became a dad, my kids were ten and five. I bypassed teething, 2:00 A.M. feedings, colic, and that toxic waste that magically appears in clean diapers. My shirts did not smell of spit-up and strained peas. I was never jarred awake by the cries of an infant who had just discovered her voice had volume. Most would say I made a good deal.

However, by missing all that, I also missed out on the recognition of being "the one" in my children's eyes. I saw it when my stepkids looked at my wife. Nathaniel, ten and too cool to show affection, melted like a snowball in August around his mom. And our five year old, Lonni, clung to her mommy like she was a security blanket.

Part of me was envious. My wife could have no more children, a fact I was aware of before we married, so I knew I would never have the chance to form that bond with a biological child of my own. I knew I would be a good father and a good dad. I had learned from infancy from the best, my own father, and I was anxious to pass on the lessons I'd learned from Dad to my children. I just didn't know if I would ever be a daddy.

My wife and her ex had split custody of the children, so my bonding time with Nathaniel was every other weekend, four weeks in the summer, and Christmas to New Year's. We became close, but in the aftermath of divorcing his mother, his father had made Nathaniel his best friend. Nathaniel's age, his closeness with his biological father, and our limited time together made it hard to make an immediate connection.

Lonni, on the other hand, took to me instantly. I went from "Mark" to "Daddy Mark" to "Daddy" in a single weekend. I taught her to swim and to ride a bike. I bathed her and read her bedtime stories and tucked her in every night. I snuck a dollar under her pillow in exchange for her first missing tooth.

Despite all this, I still didn't feel I had made it all the way to "Daddy" even with Lonni. Her natural father still got her every other weekend, and she came home from those visitations slightly withdrawn, as though she felt she was somehow being unfaithful to her father because of the way she felt for her stepfather. Before marrying their mother, I'd read everything I could on stepparenting and never tried to replace their dad. I made myself content with what I had.

Six months into our marriage, my daughter started school. The first day of kindergarten she dressed in a cute blue and white outfit and flashed a smile that couldn't have been bigger, even if she hadn't been missing two baby teeth. My wife and I drove her to school that day, stayed for orientation, and hung around until her first half day was over.

The next day, I took her to school and my wife picked her up. On day three, I dropped off and we both picked up. On day four, she wanted to ride the school bus home.

I drove her to school early that day and stopped in the office. I asked questions about the bus. I wanted to know times and locations. We lived on a winding street with no sidewalks and lots of blind spots. I wanted to confirm that the bus stopped at or near enough to our house so that Lonni would not have to walk a dangerous path. I was assured and reassured that the driver would take care of everything.

School let out at 2:45. The bus was scheduled in our neighborhood at 3:15. By three, I was on our front stoop waiting. The bus didn't show up at 3:15 or 3:20 or 3:25. By 3:30, I was on the phone to the school. They connected me with the company that ran school buses for the district, who had to route my call to the subcontractor for my daughter's bus. It had never occurred to me when I was talking to people at the school that there even were subcontractors. I had placed my daughter's safety in the hands of the school. They, in turn, had placed her safety in the hands of the bus company with the lowest bid.

Irrational panic started to set in. Intellectually, I knew the bus companies were thoroughly investigated by the school district. I knew the drivers were all vetted professionals who took child care very seriously. Intellectually, I knew this. Emotionally, I was a wreck. And the inability of anyone from the school or the bus company to tell me exactly where my daughter was did not help my growing frustration.

Finally, I saw a glimpse of the bright yellow bus through the trees and waited anxiously as it approached our house. I could see there was only one child on board. My child. I ran to the road as the bus started flashing red and stopped in front of me. The door opened and Lonni leapt out and into my arms. She hugged me harder than I had ever been hugged before. She was trying to talk to me, but she was also crying, and all that came out was a series of deep breaths, like a swimmer just saved from drowning.

"It's okay, Munchkin. You're home, everything is okay," I reassured her.

Through the tears and the hyperventilation Lonni managed one word: "Daddy."

The driver put the bus in park and stood on the top step.

"It was her first time on the bus. I didn't have her address and she couldn't remember it. I tried to let her off at the stop down the street, but she didn't know where she was, so we just kept driving around the subdivision until she saw you. She screamed 'That's my Daddy!' And we stopped. Sorry if we scared you."

I tried to answer, but I couldn't. The combination of those little arms wrapped around my neck and the beating of my heart against hers made words impossible.

We both learned something that day about something other than bus routes. Lonni learned that I was, like her mother, a safe place, a place where nothing bad would happen to her. And I learned, after months of fatherhood, what it was to be a daddy.

—*Mark Best*

# Stardust and Paper Moons

The young bandleader closed the lid of his trumpet case as his milky-blue eyes scanned the smoke-filled ballroom one last time before heading home. My daddy, Johnny McCoy, had been on the road with his big band orchestra for almost six months of engagements, traveling throughout Virginia, West Virginia, Kentucky, and Ohio. He looked forward to spending a few days with his family before hitting the road again.

Daddy's visits weren't long enough or frequent enough for my mama. But even though she bore the burden of raising my brother and me alone, she understood his life's dream of one day becoming a famous bandleader and making a name for himself. Daddy had his trumpet and his music, and with these he passionately carried the torch of the Swing Era on into the 1950s. I doubt that he stopped to think much about the pain that Mama kept masked behind her beautiful face. As for me, I didn't know any better; I was only two years old.

While the familiar tunes that Daddy performed for a living played on the radio during his drive home, the aspiring musician's thoughts of his wife and kids propelled him forward. He couldn't wait to hold Mama in his arms again and sit in his armchair with his son on his lap. The boy would surely be an inch taller. And what about his baby girl? Babies change so quickly. Daddy could think of me only in terms of the way I'd looked the last time he'd seen me six months earlier. He could almost feel the touch of my nose nuzzled into his cheek and my little arms squeezed tightly around his neck. A smile on his face, he tapped his fingers against the steering wheel in rhythm to the music of Duke Ellington and Tommy Dorsey, knowing he'd be home with his family soon.

"Daddy's here!" Mama called to my brother.

Daddy parked the car, and Kenny flew out the front door to give him the biggest bear hug ever. Mama stood on the porch, smiling through tears at the trumpet man, her emotions running the gamut from sorrow to joy. Sorrow in the brevity of her time with him and joy at having him home for a while.

Daddy's breath caught at the sight of her standing there. I slept all the way through this tearful reunion, oblivious to the profound effect that Daddy's presence had on Mama and my brother.

After Kenny and Daddy did some "catching up," Mama brought Daddy into my room to peek at me while I slept. His heart became instant mush as he stroked my soft little head. He couldn't wait for me to wake up from my nap so that we could do some father-daughter bonding.

"She's grown so much," he said. "I can't tell you how often I've tried to imagine what she looks like now. I'd think about my baby girl and remember her green eyes."

My father's presence beside my crib did nothing to stir me awake. Unlike my brother, I hadn't been waiting anxiously for his return home. After six months, in my two-year-old mind, I wasn't even aware that there was another member of our family. He'd been gone for long stretches before, but this was the longest. Mama had frequently put the phone to my ear so that I could listen to his voice, but I was too young to make any association. She also said that she had shown me pictures of him, teaching me to call the man in the photograph "Daddy." But the word and the image didn't register with me as representing a living human being.

When I finally did wake up, my mother carried me into the room, where my beaming daddy waited eagerly to greet me. Naively thinking that their little girl would be overjoyed to see her daddy, my parents were woefully unprepared for what happened next. Their smiles turned upside-down in a flash as I burst into tears and pushed myself away from my daddy with my small fists. Screaming, I ran with fright to my mother and held tightly to her, burying my face against her neck, refusing to let go. Daddy was crushed.

"Let's not push her," he said. "She'll come to me when she's ready."

He kept his distance as my mother tried to convince me that he was okay, that he was my daddy.

"You've been away from her for too long," Mama reminded him. "She's too young to handle sudden changes in her routine. She doesn't know who you are."

The words stung. And the situation didn't improve at all for the duration of his brief visit. Time after time, Daddy would try to warm up to me, try to make friends. But I wouldn't have anything to do with him.

I was unaware of the conversations between my parents during this particular visit—discussions about their marriage, about Daddy's relationship with me and my brother, about his career. His heart was being pulled in a hundred different directions and he felt like he'd completely lost control of his life. His marriage was fragile, and he needed to seriously reconsider his goals. But the heartstring that tugged the hardest was the one connected to me—his baby girl. He wanted so desperately for his daughter to believe in him, as any father would. The rejection had given him a whole new perspective on his purpose in life.

When he left, I still clung to my mother, eyeing the strange man with distrust and refusing to speak to him. He carried the weight of this less-than-affectionate farewell with him every moment during his orchestra's next set of engagements. On many a lonely night, he would stare up at a starlit sky as images of my terrified face haunted the memory of his last visit home. He tried in vain to remember me as the happy little infant I was before, now only a "stardust melody" he held inside.

One night, with the gig over and the dance floor cleared, Daddy lingered at the bar before going back to his hotel room. Seldom one to drink, he sipped a scotch on the rocks and did some deep soul-searching. Life on the road was hard, but at the same time, it was a thrill. Johnny McCoy was going to "make it" some day. At what cost, though? He shook off his blue mood and stepped outside to walk to the hotel. Glancing up at the moon in the midnight sky, these lyrics from the popular tune "Paper Moon" floated across his mind: ". . . But it wouldn't be make-believe if you believed in me." Without his family's love, life began to feel artificial, like a paper moon.

As the days and nights wore on, my father became more and more aware of the vast disconnect between himself and his family. He began to realize that he'd probably never be able to have it both ways. The name "Johnny McCoy" right up there with Stan Kenton, Harry James, Tommy Dorsey, and all the other big names of Big Band Jazz? Or would it be Johnny McCoy, devoted husband and father whose wife and children adored him?

I'm not sure exactly how long this went on. Weeks? Months, maybe? But Johnny McCoy finally did come home—to stay. He took a permanent job as a different kind of bandleader, a high school band director, while maintaining the Johnny McCoy Orchestra for local weekend gigs. Daddy no longer had to rely on the "stardust of a song" to nurture family memories.

In time, I grew to accept his presence in our home as though he'd never been gone, and the father-daughter bond he'd so longed for soon evolved into something much more authentic than paper moons.

Growing up in the home of a jazz musician was exciting: sitting in nightclubs next to Mama on Saturday nights and summer-long stays in fun-filled vacation spots where Daddy's orchestra was booked for the season. We were thrilled to be a part of this bandleader's profession, though he'd given up fame and fortune to make it possible.

The sacrifice my father made for his family may have gone without recognition from me for many years, but eventually I realized the magnanimity of the choice he'd had to make. What kind of love would drive a man to give up so much? To turn his back on his own ambitions? A father's love.

—Judy Gerlach

# Home Is Where the Hero Is

As a sports columnist, I am often asked who my hero is. The expected reply, of course, is Tiger Woods or LeBron James or Peyton Manning or Lance Armstrong, or any one of a hundred other sports superstars I've met and interviewed. But none of them is my hero.

That is not to say my hero is not an athlete. Truth is, he was a two-sport letterman in college.

Once, during a jump ball at the free-throw line at his end of the basketball court, my hero soared up and tipped the ball into the basket for two points! Even Michael Jordan has never done that.

He also possessed a hook shot that was twice the threat of Kareem Abdul-Jabbar's skyhook in that my hero shot his ambidextrously, swinging left, then right, left, right, like a windshield wiper gone berserk. As I remember it, it was as unstoppable as a rising tide.

And you know what? My hero was even better at football. A 6-foot-3-inch, 210-pound (big in his day) defensive end, he played in an era when helmets were made of leather and facemasks hadn't been invented yet. How tough was he? My hero once had his nose broken during a game, jogged over to the sidelines to have the team trainer—*crack!*—straighten the crook out of it and stuff some cotton in it to stop the bleeding, and then went back into the game a couple plays later.

He also threw a perfect spiral, with the nose of the ball pointed slightly up, the way Hall-of-Famer Otto Graham always did because that made it easier for his Browns receivers. My hero must have passed for 100,000 yards in the dark after dinner to his three favorite wideouts, all pretending to be Paul Warfield. Indeed, no matter how tired he was when he came home from work, never once can I ever remember my hero saying no when he was asked to come outside and play quarterback, or catch, or two-on-two hoops in the driveway, or tennis, or simply to play.

And isn't that what heroes do: always answer the call?

Heroes are also brave. My hero served in World War II as part of "The Greatest Generation." Enough said.

Many folks define "hero" as someone who saves lives. Well, although my hero doesn't wear a FDNY cap, he has spent most of his life saving lives, first as a lifeguard at a dangerous but popular lake and then as an emergency room surgeon, where he saved many, many more.

It should come as no surprise, then, that I have never seen my hero panic. Joe Montana was cool in a two-minute drill, but real pressure is cutting open a chest and trying to find out where the bleeding is coming from before too many precious seconds tick away. It certainly puts "deadline pressure" for writing a story in proper perspective.

A true hero also needs a heart. I have seen my hero shed tears for lives he couldn't save. When a new friend of mine casually mentioned his father had died a few years ago, my hero began including him in weekend outings and even bought him a pair of sneakers that were more expensive and cool than the ones he would buy my two brothers and me. "You have a father, he doesn't," my hero explained.

When I was very little, perhaps five years old, I remember my hero studying for his medical boards at the kitchen table as I headed off to bed. And I remember getting up in the middle of the night to get a glass of water to see him still there studying. Perhaps that is why pulling all-nighters in college and working late nights in press boxes has never bothered me.

Growing up, I hung posters of Jerry West and Stan Smith and Gale Sayers and Johnny Bench on my bedroom wall. But I never hung up a poster of my hero. I didn't need to. Instead of being pictured on the box of Wheaties, my hero sat next to me at the breakfast table each morning.

Even these days, after the events of September 11 and with our country at war in Afghanistan and Iraq, pro athletes are still often heralded as heroes. But do you know who many sports superstars say their hero is? . . . Their dads. Magic Johnson says it. Shaquille O'Neal says it. John Wooden says it.

That puts me in good—and blessed—company.

My hero turned eighty-one last Thanksgiving day. Before dinner, I asked him to toss the football to me a few times. I'm happy to say my hero still throws a perfect spiral, maybe not as far as he once did, but as easy to catch as ever with the nose of the ball pointed slightly up. Indeed, for a few moments, I felt ten again.

—*Woody Woodburn*

# Tattoos of the Heart

He pulled up his shirt sleeve to reveal the letters: K–A–T–H–Y.

"I never forgot about you," he said.

My eyes followed the lines of each letter. It was one of those homemade tattoos, the kind your buddy gives you after you've both had a few too many.

What could I say? My parents split up and my father left town when I was just a year old. Since then, I'd been protecting myself, not willing to attach emotionally to a man who wouldn't be there. He did call a few times when I was very young, always promising he'd be in town for a visit soon. But he never showed up.

I remember sitting on a bench during recess in the fifth grade. We had just finished creating our family trees in class.

A friend came up to me and asked, "Why do you act like you don't care about your dad?"

"Because he doesn't care about me," I said, jutting out my chin. "He walked out on us. Why should I care?"

My friend looked down at the ground, kicking the sand around with her toe. "Oh, I guess you're right," she said. She walked away, glancing back over her shoulder.

Without my dad around to help, my mother worked a second-shift job to support us. At twelve, I was responsible for cooking and feeding dinner to my younger sister, helping her with her homework, and tucking her into bed at night. It just didn't seem fair.

My mom died when I was fourteen. After that, my sister and I lived with my grandmother. This would've been the perfect time for my dad to come around again. But he didn't. I was alone.

As I grew older, I longed for my dad even more. I had few male relatives around and none that I really looked up to as a parenting role model. As a teenager, I searched for that father figure in all the wrong places. I dated older guys and gave away my innocence long before I was ready. At eighteen, I moved in with my twenty-nine-year-old boyfriend. I married him when I was twenty-two. Within three years, my husband was unemployed, chronically drunk, and facing felony drug charges. My quest to use him to fill the role of daddy had gone seriously wrong. I left him with only my car and a few garbage bags full of clothes. I was more alone than ever and sought refuge at an uncle's house. I cried myself to sleep many times over the next several weeks.

Determined to make it on my own, I forged ahead. In less than three months, I had my own apartment and my self-respect. I could, and would, make it on my own, I told myself and everyone around me. I was pretty tough on the outside.

But underneath my tough exterior, I still yearned for my daddy.

One year after my divorce was final, my father decided to call. Not me; he called my uncle. My uncle gave me the message along with my dad's contact information so I could call him back. At twenty-six, I wasn't sure I wanted to call him back. I'd made it this far without him. I buried the slip of paper in one of my junk boxes at home and pushed the message out of my mind. Or tried to. Like a persistent fruit fly, it wouldn't leave me alone.

Finally, after about four months, half-hoping he just might care about me, I picked up the phone. "I'm calling for Frank Adams," I said to the unfamiliar voice that answered.

"This is Frank."

"Uh, hi . . . Frank." The word "Dad" got stuck in my throat. "This is Kathy. Uncle Don gave me your number."

"That's right. I called him a while back to see how you was doin'."

"Uh, listen, I just need your address. I need to send you something," I blurted, not quite sure where those words came from or what I might send him.

I jotted down the address, quickly ended the call, and hung up the phone. Then crumpled into a chair, my heart thumping wildly in my chest. It may have been just a voice on the phone, but it was my father's voice.

What was I thinking, saying I needed to send him something with no idea of what I would send? Then I remembered: his birthday was the next month; I could send a birthday card.

A few days later, I stood anxiously looking through a rack of birthday cards. None of the messages seemed quite right. My father hadn't "been there for me" growing up. He'd never taken me fishing or helped me with my homework. He hadn't spoken words of wisdom to me or showered me with fatherly affection. Finally, I grabbed a generic card off the shelf. I scribbled my name—just my name, with no "Love" before it—and hesitantly added my phone number before sending it off. Expecting nothing in return.

But he did call. And after more than a few awkward telephone conversations, we settled into a comfortable telephone relationship. We talked at every major holiday and occasionally at other times throughout the year.

I remarried in 2001, and my daughter was born in March 2003. After her birth, I reflected on the relationship I had with my own father. Consumed by a desire to take it to the next level, I decided to go visit him. My husband, my daughter, and I flew from our home in Wisconsin to South Carolina, where my father lived.

The airport was tiny, and the airplane landed a short distance from the airport. I felt light-headed as I walked toward the terminal, my mind racing. *What was I thinking? What would he do when he saw us? Was this even the right thing to do?* But it was too late to turn back now.

As soon as we entered the airport, I saw him. I knew instantly it was him. Average build, mousy brown hair parted on the side and combed down with grease. His wife, a short and not-so-pleasingly plump woman stood next to him. Eyeing us up, she said, "I tol' Frank, we just need to look for a white woman, a black man, and a yella' baby."

My father stood there silently with his hands thrust deep into his pockets. He appeared to be just as uncomfortable as I was.

"Hey, Pops," my husband said, extending his hand to my father. Leave it to my husband to break an awkward moment.

After a quick hello, we focused on locating our luggage from the baggage claim area. With bags in tow, we followed my dad and his wife outside and loaded up in the back of his raggedy, late-model, red Thunderbird.

We spent three days in South Carolina. Most of the time, we hung out at their house, a two-bedroom trailer where my dad lived with his wife and mother-in-law. There was no real driveway or even a lawn, just gravel and some scattered crab grass that wasn't really trying to grow. An old rusty shed stood next to the trailer.

"It ain't much, I reckon," my dad liked to say, "but it's paid fer."

In spite of our history and the racist culture of the deep southern town, my father welcomed us with open arms. Townspeople, and even some relatives, gave us dirty looks and turned away when they realized we were together.

"I want to sit down and talk wit' you," he said several times during our visit.

Each time, he shared a snippet of his history and the man he was. Uneducated and illiterate but hardworking, he'd driven a semi tractor-trailer most of his life. On the road for weeks at a time, he relied on fellow truckers to help him fill out the logbooks he couldn't read for himself.

And while he hadn't been there for me physically or emotionally, in his mind, he'd never stopped loving me.

Four years after we visited him, my father ventured north to spend a few weeks with my family. It was one of the worst winters we'd had in Wisconsin in a while, with record snowfalls. Yet, he drove for three days in the same raggedy red Thunderbird, conquering icy highways and drifting snow along the way to get here.

And now here he was, sitting on the sofa in my family room, both hands wrapped tightly around the coffee cup in his hand. The brutality of a lifetime showed in the lines of his face, the regrets of his choices in his eyes.

I traced the letters on his shoulder again: K–A–T–H–Y.

"I never forgot about you, either," I said.

—*Kathy L. Adams McIntosh*

# Battle of the Bulging Eyes

A sudden piercing shriek ripped through the wall of my bedroom. My protective paternal instinct kicked in as I pounced out of bed, stumbled down the hall, and crashed into my daughter's room. I'm not sure what I expected, but it had to be big and bad. Whatever had made my sweet angel cry out with such terror had to be horrible. Terrifying. Evil. My imagination went wild. Perhaps someone was looming over her—a ruddy overweight abductor in clown makeup and big floppy shoes. He must have followed her home, drawn by the scent of salty French fry grease on her lips after our special Daddy/Daughter date at the drive-through.

I took the distance between my angel's doorway and her princess bed in one giant leap. Her sweet face was contorted, eyes as large as the moon that hung in the midnight blue outside her window. Tears washed down both of her cheeks onto the ruffled pink duvet. I snapped my head around for a quick survey. Where was the clown who would dare try to abduct my baby?

"Spider," she said in a tiny petrified whisper.

I must have looked confused.

She whispered the word again, a faint "spider," as though the creature might hear her and lunge for her.

I knew that word. Eight creepy-crawly legs, billions of beady eyes, black, hairy, deadly poisonous. I nodded once and began the daunting task of The Spider Hunt. My angel's panicked breathing slowed as she watched me search for the elusive beast.

My search began along the north perimeter, over by the glowing red embers of the digital clock. I tipped the double-bubble pink dresser away from the wall, eyes darting, scanning for a speck of black. Black. This creature of the night was usually black with a blood-red violin marking on its back. But the fiend was not hiding behind the dresser. Good thing; I had gained a bit of weight. There was no way I'd have been able to gallantly reach back there and squash my foe. Well, I may have been able to get in, but getting out would have required a 9-1-1 call, a fire truck filled with firefighters, the jaws of life, and fifteen minutes of fame on the local 6:00 news.

Under the bed! With great flourish, I manipulated my daughter's flower-shaped flashlight to sweep the lost zone under her bed. Scary dust bunnies swayed to the beat of some unknown wind source. Something that looked like a lollipop with fur on it stared back at me like a lost eyeball. No spider.

With very little grace or agility I wobbled up from my knees and looked at my angel. Blanket up to her nose, eyes closed.

I announced in a hushed whisper, "He's gone."

Then I inched my way out of the room and shut the door. Back in my cold bed, I pulled the cover up to my chin and shut my eyes. Proud of myself, with another disaster averted, I soon began to dream about receiving the Father of the Year Award from the President.

Shriek! Louder than before. This time it *was* an intruder. The clown was in her room, tying her up with duct tape and bubble wrap.

I raced to her room, switched on the overhead light, and struck my best kung fu stance.

"Spider, Daddy! Spider!"

Okay, that was it. The tormenter would be mine! I looked under a pile of pony books. I poked into her Barbie stash, every doll in that box returning my crazed gaze, eyes wide with terror, limbs rigid with fright. I shuffled through her stack of stuffies. I looked for footprints in the dust under her princess clock. I ducked inside her closet—a blinding flash of pink cotton blend, lace, and sparkles—and scoured its depths, looking for the little heathen. No spider. But I did find my cell phone case, with Rainbow Pony nesting comfortably inside.

Again, I made the announcement: "Spider has left the building."

After kissing my angel gently on the forehead, I crept back to my room and fell into bed. Switched off the light. But not my mind.

*Of course, Spider was gone. How could anything that big be so elusive? Certainly, I was the smarter of we two; look at the brain-mass ratio.*

A single strand of hair stood erect at my nape.

*He was in here, watching me. He was waiting for me to fall asleep so he could walk all over my face, some sick sort of spider samba. Maybe it wasn't a he; maybe it was an egg-laden female, waiting to make her nest in my ear.*

I snapped on the light on and looked for the she-beast along the cobweb-lined ceiling.

Another ear-splitting shriek slammed the dry-wall between our rooms. This time, *all* the hairs on my neck stood up. This was no ordinary spider! It must be massive, with long black hairs bristling along its razor-pointed legs. And huge antennae—

big as antlers—perched over its bulging black eyes. And foot-long fang things poking out of its gaping maw, covered in digestive juice, oozing onto the rug. And a massive throbbing thorax covered in stiff prickly fur wagging in anticipated attack. And I was sure this monster was poised over my daughter ready to rip into her pale-pink-icing colored blankie.

I kicked her door open, grabbed two of her Barbies and faced them pointed feet out, ready to pierce the underbelly of the beast, ready to give my life for my baby girl.

"Spider," she sobbed, pointing. "Spider, spider spider!"

And there it was: a tiny pin spot on the wall, a speck of dust, really. It moved. Slowly, I lowered the Barbie dolls and placed them in front of me. With hands held open, I backed away.

I knew what I had to do, what was the right thing for such a worthy opponent. This cunning enemy had earned my respect, my admiration even. I took a tissue from the tissue box. My daughter grinned with glee at the thought of her knight in shining armor extinguishing the beast that had invaded her kingdom. But her grin quickly faded when she realized what I was about to do to her tiny terrorist.

"Aren't you gonna kill it?" she asked.

"Even better, my princess," I assured her. "I will banish her from your castle forevermore."

I placed the soft, white tissue ahead of the spider, and she climbed aboard. With care I ferried the venomous man-hunter to the front door and put the tissue on the ground outside. I saluted my enemy as she marched off into the night. With a deep sigh, I shut the door and went back to my angel's room. I kissed her peaceful eyelids and the proud smile on her lips, then went off to my own bed. With not a single drop of blood shed, I was a true hero. Finally, with covers pulled up to my chin, I drifted off to dreamland, where the President bestowed me with the coveted Father of the Year Award.

—*Libby Kennedy as told by Tom Kennedy*

# To Kayla:
# With Love, Daddy

This is my fourth Father's Day message to you. It has been an eventful year of swinging at the playground, hide and seek, books and more books, and many blessed moments of snuggles and cuddles. You discovered sweets, and you are fond of them. I am amazed at how you can take an Oreo cookie and five minutes later look like you have been dipped in a vat of chocolate fudge. I am even more amazed at the fascinating little person you have become.

Thinking about this past year of fatherhood reminds me of when we tracked people's footprints along a sandy beach. I suggested how tall that person must have been based on the size of the print. You asked me what they were wearing.

While you dug for dinosaurs in the moist sand, I tried to process what is pressed into your psyche every day from sources so abundant it befuddles comprehension. What first impressions will all these new concepts leave upon your young mind, absorbent as a sponge in the ocean? I realize that many of those notions will adhere together and take creative form unrecognizable from their origin, like barnacles adhesively piled on top of one another. I am a little frightened by the prospect of not being able to control what sticks and what washes away. But I also find myself smiling at glittering possibilities as I reflect upon how you put your thoughts together, even at the age of three.

So, when we sit in our small bathroom, you on the little potty and me on the adult-sized commode, facing and leaning toward one another, hands clasped like two ball players awaiting final instructions from our coach, I am always curious about the conversation that may be forthcoming. I can almost feel the heat of the ideas burning in your head, and I eagerly anticipate a new message.

Finally ready, you turn your saucer blue eyes up toward me and in a whisper, "I love you, Daddy."

The lingering beauty of this moment is that I realize you really mean it, and it seems like a gift from God. I feel both joy and responsibility bestowed upon me by what you have said and only slightly off-balance, knowing your pool of dads to compare me with is virtually nonexistent. To still be me and to help you develop feels awesome at times. I can't even claim I'm doing my best. I can say only that I am very aware and hope history provides evidence of my positive presence in your life.

"I love you, too, Kayla," I reply.

As Mommy and I look forward to your fourth year of life, I am proud to say I have seen you express both humanity and humor in your third.

"Bless you!" shouts a small squeaky voice from your bedroom.

"Bless you," the cry comes again in response to my allergy-laden, AK–47 machine-gun sneezing.

You appear at your doorway, turn your head toward the living room, where I'm sitting on the couch, and fix your eyes upon my tissue-covered face.

"Are you okay, Daddy?"

"I think I'll make it," I manage to say before firing off another round.

We both have allergies. Yours are manifested more through a seasonally stuffy nose, which causes you to snore in a manner that would surely keep coyotes at bay if we ever go camping.

At present, Mom or I sleep with you every night. Occasionally, we race each other for the privilege; sometimes, I think your mother lets me win. There is always a pile of books on the nightstand, usually ones you have carefully selected earlier in the evening.

As you settle in with your bottle, we lie side by side, giving your fingers easy access to my left ear to squeeze and wiggle, which, for reasons known only to you, provides comfort and helps you wind down. You are attentive through *Barney's Book of Opposites*, but halfway through *The Runaway Bunny*, I know your focus is elsewhere and I turn off the lamp. As my eyes adjust in the hazy darkness, I stare for a while at the dresser near the foot of our bed. Atop it rests an oval-shaped beveled mirror anchored by slender, swirly strands of oak. I am sure this looking glass must be similar to the one Alice went through to discover the wonders of a Mad Hatter and the dangers posed by a Queen of Hearts.

I think about the scrapes on your knees: the one on your right still chipped with brownish crust and the two on your left, a healthy pink and healing nicely. When you were one and newly mobile, I actually made a commitment to protect you always against scraped knees and all other owies. This year you have demonstrated time and again what folly that was on my part. Although unrealistic, I still cannot relinquish the plan. I want to protect you always. I want to go, too, when you go through the looking glass.

I mentioned humor before, and although you are not quite ready for the stage, you are definitely an entertainer. "The Alphabet Song" is tops in your repertoire. The letters are never far from your mind, and you sing them constantly. I have yet to tire of your rendition.

But when you did your first joke last November, I really knew, most assuredly, that you were my child. I was poking at your mom while she was trying to do the dishes and I was talking about clowning around. During the action, you slipped off to the bedroom and moments later came bursting into the kitchen stark naked except for your Halloween clown hat, circled us rapidly like Shriners do in parades, and sprinted off again. Pun-ish humor like that can only be derived from my genetic stream. I could not have been prouder if you had hit one out of the ballpark.

Even more astounding than your humor, though, is your wisdom. Immediately following the practical application of a hypothesis I did not realize you had been formulating, you made the following announcement with great and compelling certainty in your voice: "If you're itchy, Daddy, you should itch."

Now, if those aren't words to live by, I don't know what are.

—*Samuel P. Clark*

*This story was first published in* Parents Today,
*June 1998.*

# Papa's Gold Coin

Whenever my father spoke of loyalty or tradition or parental respect, he would always tell the story of the gift his grandmother gave him in 1915 when he was a child of ten years old. For dramatic effect, he would stand up, hold out his hand toward us, his index finger and thumb pressed together, and say in a strong, emotional voice, "Even if I were starving and didn't have any money to buy food, I would never sell this coin my grandmother gave me!"

We children—there were six of us—tried hard to get a good look at that coin. Papa's hand was waving now; it was hard to see between his two fingers. He was like one of those magicians playing the all-time favorite coin trick where first you see it and then you don't. It added to the impact of his story. Papa loved drama. If a tale could be told in a matter of several quick sentences, he would draw it out, pause now and then for the benefit of suspense, and add just enough hand gestures and facial expressions to keep his audience alert and interested.

"Pa," said my sister Joanie, "can we look at it?"

Anna, the oldest of the girls, chimed in, "Yeah, we want to see that money your grandma gave!"

Papa smiled, then brought his hand under our noses and revealed to us that between his index finger and his thumb was nothing but air! He laughed so loud to see us searching the table and then the floor to find the coin that had mysteriously disappeared.

"Where did it go, Pa?" we all wanted to know.

How did he one minute hold it in his hand and the next make it vanish into the kitchen air?

Then Papa's face grew serious again. He opened his hand the way that proverbial magician I mentioned will do when he is ready to reveal you have been duped by a master. "See the coin?" he asked us.

"No, Pa. Where did it go?" asked Sarah.

"How did you do that?" older brother Al asked.

Then Papa sat in his favorite table chair again, a sign he would finish his story or begin a new one—another lesson we needed to learn in life about giving and receiving. But he called it not story, but "parable."

"You don't see the coin because I keep it hidden," he said. We gave him that question-mark look by knitting our eyebrows.

He raised his hand in case one of us intended to interrupt him. "What if I lost it? What if it fell from my fingers, rolled somewhere and was lost forever?

"I lost a dime once," Sarah said. Annoyed with her interruption, I said, "You probably bought candy and want another dime now." But when Sarah started crying, I was sorry I'd said that.

Papa put his hand in his pocket and brought out a dime and handed it to Sarah.

"A dime!" he said. "What's a dime, anyway? So many of them you can lose one and find one in the same few minutes. But the coin my mother gave me . . . Oh, that was something different than a dime. It was made of pure gold."

We looked at one another. A gold coin? We had heard and read about pirates and gold treasures, but in real life? Papa must have read our minds.

"Real gold," he said. "A five-dollar piece with the date of 1883."

Here we were in 1954. "That's really old," I said.

Meanwhile, Joanie was counting on her fingers how many years had gone by since that gold coin was brand new. Finally, she called out, "Seventy-one years!"

Papa nodded. "It was the year my grandfather Giovanni died. My grandmother gave me that gold coin, not to spend, but to save someplace safe."

"Why didn't she give it to your father?" seemed like a logical question for me to ask. After all, wouldn't Grandpa be a little offended if his own mother preferred to give such a valuable gift to her grandson and not her own son? It just didn't make sense.

Now Papa looked sad. There he was, all prepared to deliver his parable that somehow revolved around this gold coin, and one of us had thrown in a monkey wrench, derailing his plans. I looked at Mama, who had left the sink where she was drying dinner dishes to sit at the table beside Papa. Her face took on that same sadness. *What gives?* I wondered.

When Papa lifted his head, we could all see the mist in his dark brown eyes. His lips were tight beneath his dark moustache until he began to speak. Then they trembled, the words coming out of his mouth so whisperingly low we had to pull our chairs closer to hear him. Now and then, choked up with emotion, he raised his hand to indicate he was pausing again. You could not hear a sound in that silent Brooklyn kitchen of so long ago.

And we kids eyed one another, wondering what had brought this on. What terribly sad thing had caused our father, our family's pillar of strength, to all at once fight off tears? I thought of only yesterday when I had skinned my knee on the pavement and came limping upstairs, crying my eyes out. Mama had looked at the abrasion, took burning peroxide to it with a handkerchief, and dabbed away while I continued to grit my teeth and cry.

Just then Papa had called from the living room, "Big boys don't waste their time with tears. Your knee can take it. Just be careful next time."

Now it was Papa, champion of the stiff upper lip, on the verge of tears.

At last Papa's hand came down to the table and he began to speak. "She gave it to me because my father was gone."

When we expressed wonder as to what "gone" meant, Mama clarified by adding, "He died."

Now Papa was standing again. He was taking his parable-time pose with which we were all so familiar. What lesson was in the making? What would he tell us about the death of his father?

"I had an older brother once," he began. "He was the first one named like me—Michael, after my mother's father, Michael Pitonzo. Of course, I never knew him. He was born in 1883."

"Like the gold coin," Sarah piped in.

"The same year your grandpa died!" I said.

"Like the coin. Like my grandpa," echoed Papa. "The first Michael was a very talented shoemaker."

At that, we started laughing; we couldn't help it. We knew the old shoemaker Signor Alaimo, whose shop was a few doors down on Graham Avenue, and in our minds his work and the word "talent" did not go hand in hand. He took nails from where he kept them clenched between his lips, taking them out one at a time to hammer into a new heel and sole, hammering away like one of Santa's elves. *What's the talent in that?* seemed to be the unspoken question around the table.

"No," Papa explained. "He didn't repair shoes; he made them from scratch. Took leather and shaped it to fit someone's feet, so that when that person walked it was like walking on air.

"Anyway, this brother Michael was his father's pride and joy, even though, at the time, he also had a son named Giovanni and two daughters, Serafina and Ninetta."

Sarah's eyes lit up. My parents had named her after Papa's oldest sister.

"Still, it was Michael who seemed to hold so much promise. He was only seventeen, and already he'd invented a shoemaking tool that made the job easier. My father was so proud of him that he sent him to a shoe-design school in the capital city of Palermo. Michael left his little Sicilian village and went to Palermo, where he got very sick . . ." Papa paused again to catch his breath or to swallow the rising tears in his throat, we weren't sure which.

Then he continued. "My father would visit him

each week and find his son getting worse and worse. They said he had gangrene. Maybe it was cancer. Who knows? The sickness was spreading. Each visit, my father would find the sickness had taken another limb from his son. They amputated a leg, an arm, the other leg. Michael would beg his father not to come anymore because it made his father so sad. But my papa would not listen. 'You are my son,' I suppose he would tell him, 'and I love you!'

"To make a long, sad story short, Michael died at eighteen years old. That was in 1902. I was born in 1905, the last of my parents' ten children. And my father? He couldn't go back to the happy man he once was. The death of his son took everything out of him. When I was only six months old, my Papa died of a broken heart."

The table grew quiet again. We had learned about our Uncle Michael and our Grandfather Alfonso from Papa, who kept so many stories inside him that it amazed us.

No one said anything for what seemed a long time. Then Papa, with complete composure again, returned to the parable of the gold coin.

"So my grandmother gave me the gold coin. It was important that I keep it forever," he said. "In a way, it represents the man who was born in the same year as the coin was minted. And another man who died that same year. Maybe it was my grandmother's way of saying I should keep the memory of all those good men in our family alive. I know she wanted me to save the coin forever."

"Like, in a bank?" Sarah asked.

Papa shook his head and touched his heart. "Someplace safe."

We wondered if there really was a gold coin. We had never seen it. Papa kept it hidden, but if the hiding place was, as he hinted, in his heart, maybe there was no coin. Just the memory of a gold coin.

"It's not the value of the coin," Papa went on. "Some things you can't take to the store and buy stuff with, and yet they are more valuable than gold. Like people we love who leave this world. They are worth more than all the treasures you can find!"

Years later, when Papa died, my mother said he had bequeathed that gold coin to me.

"He wanted you to have it because he knew you would never spend it."

Like my father before me, I value that shiny five-dollar gold piece with its Lady Liberty on one side and the American eagle on the other far beyond its material worth. It is the best gift I have ever been given. It reminds me that love endures.

—*Salvatore Buttaci*

# Yes, Sir, Daddy,
# Darling, Sir!

On that bright September morning in 1959, the kind that sparks apples on your cheeks, we walked across the school parking lot. The brick building loomed gargantuan in front of us, and the pillared vestibule was filled to the brim with noisy kids. Some were confident, smug, smacking each other on the shoulders as if to say, "This is my place." Others bounced against their parent's hands in fidgety excitement; I was one of those.

The man holding my hand towered over my head. He had a dark complexion, abundant strands of wavy black hair (always perfectly groomed), and shining black eyes.

I glared at the other kindergartners as we approached the school, but then tucked myself behind my father's leg when they glared back. There was never a more comforting place than behind that leg.

My little arms reached around his knee and held on to still the wild drumming of my heart. His dark uniform smelled of cigarettes and dry cleaning solution. I loved that smell. This was my hero, my dad.

In his rowdy youth, Roland Charles Smith II— "Smitty" to his friends, "Sir" to everyone else—had been barnstorming in Illinois when World War II broke out and the United States Army Air Corp "recruited" him to train eighteen-year-olds to fly. He crashed a plane and ended up in the base hospital, where Hap, the beautiful red-headed editor for the camp paper, interviewed him and fell in love. They were married soon after.

This was one of my favorite stories, and I always thought of it when I was scared. It now danced in the back of my head as I watched the gangling group of children and parents begin to file into the building. Muted chatter turned to deafening echoes against the long corridors and green linoleum floors. Standing like cheerful soldiers, the teachers stood at attention outside their respective forts, each armed with a clipboard, pencil, whistle, and deep reserves of patience.

I was scared down to my toenails. Mom had to work that morning or she would have been there. I was glad it was Dad instead. My mother, a logical, pragmatic individual, always took the high road on any decision: "Buck up, Missy. It's not the end of the world." My father, on the other hand, was a human contradiction and, therefore, never boring. He had a lightning temper that fizzled almost as quickly as it left his mouth, a supersonic wit, and an anger-edged compassion that was second to none. Adversely, he also nurtured creativity, awarded intelligent solutions with high praise, and more important, could take the pain out of anything with a smile. Dad was a dichotomy of the first order.

He must have felt my hand trembling as we walked toward my kindergarten classroom, because he said, "It's going to be great, duchess. You'll love school."

I tightened my lips against the title, as I always did, and managed a feeble shrug.

Dad had pet names for four out of the five of us. My oldest brother was always just "Mikey." My sister was "princess," my second oldest brother was "buddy," I was "duchess," and my little brother (poor soul) was "dink." Dad used to tell everyone that he had wanted to name him "Whiskey" since he was the fifth but was overruled by my mother.

He squeezed my hand and herded me toward a waiting lady who was both young and beautiful. Glancing down the line of teachers, I was glad I got the prettiest one. She flashed white teeth at me. The sparkle in her eyes looked fresh and genuine;

it would fade through the year, but for now it was opening-day bright.

"Good morning," she said to my dad, obviously impressed with the major's dapper uniform and the smell of Old Spice that followed him everywhere. "I'm Mrs. Anderson." She winked at me. "And this is . . . ?"

Dad squeezed my hand again, which sent me back behind his leg to peek past the sharply creased, dark green wool. In command as always, he snaked a hand behind him and pulled me front and center, then securely rested his hands on my shoulders to keep me there.

"Don't be rude, Mimi. What do you say?"

"Sorry," I mumbled.

Dad patiently cleared his throat. "Sorry, what?"

I glanced up at the radiant young woman's face and found a measure of comfort there. "Sorry, ma'am."

"This is Mimi," my father told her, giving my shoulders a pat.

Mrs. Anderson scanned her clipboard and made a quick check mark. "Here she is."

She shot another of those admiring grins in my dad's direction and a pang of jealousy flushed my face. I liked her a little less.

With a graceful whoosh of her starched cotton skirt, Mrs. Anderson moved aside and motioned to a room full of wonders. There were toys stacked in big red bins, beautiful letters, numbers, and pictures on the wall, and scampering boys and girls everywhere, not to mention several huge unshuttered windows revealing the blustery fall weather and a grove of hazelnut trees outside.

I completely forgave her transgression when she said, "Make yourself at home, Mimi. In a little bit we'll have a story and some singing." That was good enough for me.

Dad turned me around and did something rare for him: he hunkered down so we were eye to eye. "I've got to go to the base, duchess, but Mom will be off work in time to pick you up at three," he said. "I want you to behave for Mrs. Anderson and the rest of the teachers here. Yes?"

I put my hands behind my back, sent a suspicious glance through the classroom door, and then looked at my feet. "Yes."

Dad pulled back his head. "Yes, what?" His voice had that mock sternness I had learned to love from before I could remember.

"Yes, sir, Daddy, darling, sir!" I said, then lifted my tiny hand and saluted twice. He gave me a quick hug and hustled me toward the door.

"Yes, sir, Daddy, darling, sir!" (Salute twice.) That was the defining axiom of our relationship for the twenty-two years I knew him.

Since Dad was a commanding officer in the National Guard, we weren't exactly military, but we weren't exactly civilians either. Most times, he was in our lives full-time except for one weekend a month and two weeks in the summer. The only thing that ever pulled him away from us was a major disaster, a search-and-rescue mission, or any of a number of parties that he and his pilot buddies attended at the officers' club on the base. My father was a very popular fellow.

He loved fishing, highly polished brass, electroplating, off-color jokes, and exotic birds. (He once had four Java temple birds named "Ring," "A," "Ding," and "Ding.") But most of all, he loved poker. So much so that on allowance day he would gather my little brother and me together and produce a worn deck of cards and two shiny quarters.

"Okay, kids. Here's your allowance."

As Dad mesmerized us with his fancy card handling, we would *ooo* and *ahh*, dreaming about all the penny candy we could buy with our riches. Dad would sit at the dinner table and shuffle those cards like a pro. We'd take our seats next to him and wonder again how this amazing man could be our father, ignoring the echo of my mother's admonishing voice in the background saying, "Smitty?"

He would lift one hand to her, still shuffling the cards in the other, and say jovially, "Hap, it's just penny ante. You want to join in?"

Mom would scowl at him and go back to her book and cigarette. "Here's how you play," he'd say to us. "There are thirteen cards in each suit and several hands, each worth a little more."

And so it would begin. The first few times, we would win double and sometimes triple our allowances. Those were some of the best stomachaches I ever had. Later, for some reason, I didn't win as much; in fact, I'd lose more and more each time—at least until I got older; then Dad had to work for my allowance.

Standing in the classroom doorway, I reached into my pocket and felt the reassuring handful of candy sitting there, candy I had bought with that weekend's winnings. Mom would have killed me had she known, but Dad didn't say a word when he'd helped me with my coat that morning, although I knew he'd seen them.

The children's voices shrieked down the hall, covering up Dad's retreating footsteps as he left me to fend for myself. I sort of half-stumbled and half-sauntered into class, watching to make sure no one was staring at me. They all were.

After hanging up my coat, I smoothed my brand new brown and white plaid school dress into place, found a toy, and sat down at one of the little desks at the back of the room to examine it without interest. A few minutes later, the teacher came into the classroom escorting three late arrivals, whispered to them to find a seat, and then stood before the class.

"Welcome," she said as she printed something on the blackboard. "I'm Mrs. Anderson, and this is how I spell my name. Later, we'll practice spelling your names."

The screech of the chalk sent my ears buzzing, but I was so excited it didn't bother me at all.

Mrs. Anderson read the promised story, the beginning of *The Wizard of Oz*. Then she taught us a new song about winter, which I intoned at the top of my lungs, pretending I already knew it, making up words that sounded vaguely like the lyrics. Next, we sat in a circle on the floor.

"All right, children, now we're going to see how well you can count," Mrs. Anderson announced. "How many of you can count to twenty?"

My hand shot up as high as it could go amidst the chatter of excited hopefuls.

The teacher flicked her finger toward me and said, "All right, Mimi, you go first."

Bringing myself to my full two-foot sitting height, I proudly cleared my throat and recited, "One, two, three, four, five, six, seven, eight, nine, ten, jack, queen, king."

Everything got quiet. Teacher's face went blank. The clock ticked five times. Then, all at once, the children let out a roar of laughter. I sat there confused. I must have done well if they were all so excited. I bathed in the glory of my success. The teacher lifted one side of her mouth and moved on to the next child.

That night my mother and father received a phone call. The next thing I knew, they both sat me down and explained that cards were not supposed to be used for counting and they never wanted me to do it again. I wasn't exactly sure what I wasn't supposed to do, but I promised them wholeheartedly I wouldn't. I'll never forget the look of disapproval on my mother's face squarely aimed at my poor father, who lifted the newspaper higher and gave me a surreptitious wink from behind the print as he stoked his pipe. He taught me to count properly the very next day.

Dad loved me unconditionally, saw me through the best and worst of it, sparked my irreverent soul, and set fire to my imagination with gusto. And to this day, although he's been gone thirty-two years, I still say, "Yes, sir, Daddy, darling, sir!" (Salute twice). And mean it.

—*Minnette Meador*

# Montana Bananas
## and Sure Shots

For nearly three decades, the man who would later become my husband was a card room manager or dealer in Reno, Nevada. Harold's Club, Circus Circus, Nugget, Primadonna, Sundowner—Ken had worked them all. At one time he even ran his own school for aspiring dealers of Texas hold 'em and seven card stud, teaching such esoteric techniques as "high low splits." When I met him in 1999, the vanity plate on his car read "Bettor."

So I moved slowly into the relationship, hesitant about getting involved with a gambler. But, to my surprise, I soon learned that Ken had little interest in betting himself, and none of his three adult sons, all reared in this fabled "Greatest Little City in the World" had ever taken to gambling.

"Wasn't it difficult for them growing up in Reno to resist the glamour and glitz of the casinos?" I asked. As a clinical social worker in Los Angeles, in an era before the advent of World Series of Poker showdowns and omnipresent Indian casinos, I had commiserated with families whose teens were hooked on gambling, even with the relative paucity of venues in the Southland.

"I thought about that when the boys were starting elementary school," Ken told me. "So, early on, I promised myself that I would teach them everything I knew, including how to figure odds and the percentages."

He taught them checkers and chess, Tripoli, and Monopoly as well as how to ride a bike, how to cook, and later, how to drive. He also taught them everything he knew about card games, emphasizing that the odds always, always, *always* favor the house. There were no sure shots.

In his work in the casinos, Ken routinely heard tales from colleagues and customers about how they had squandered their paychecks on slots or blackjack. When he dealt, he, indeed, had to keep a poker face to avoid laughing aloud when the self-proclaimed wagering wizards at his table would brag to one another about how they were going to make a killing, even as they were losing yet another hand.

Aware that attitudes toward gambling tend to evolve in childhood, Ken was ever vigilant for telltale signs that his sons might fall prey. By early adolescence, the boys had begun to taunt one another with bets:

"I can run around the block faster than you."

"Can not."

"Can too! Wanna bet?"

Wearying of this banter, Ken designed a ploy he hoped would put an end to it. Each week, when he doled out their allowances, he would devise a sucker bet to win it back before the boys could spend it.

One evening, he came home from his shift and found the boys tossing cards at a spaghetti pot. Scott, the oldest, was the current champ, with about a dozen cards finding their mark.

"I'll bet you all a quarter that I can toss in forty," Ken boasted.

Of course, the boys took the bet—and then watched in amazement as their dad stuffed the cards back into the box and tossed in the whole pack.

Ken ignored their plaintive cries of "not fair" as he collected his winnings.

He had made his point: gambling isn't fair, and the odds always favor the house.

One Sunday morning, the boys gathered in the kitchen for breakfast and Ken bet them that he could make a raw egg float to the top of a pot of cold water.

"That's impossible," they chorused, digging in their pockets for their coins.

Ken opened a carton, plucked out an egg, and placed it in the pot of water, where it promptly sunk to the bottom. Then he reached for a container of salt and added its contents. With increased water density, the egg slowly floated to the top. The boys paid off once again.

Finally, after one example after another, Ken thought the boys had finally learned their lesson. But one evening he came home from work to find the middle son, Rick, sitting on the sofa, pointing to a set of headphones propped against the stereo.

"Dad, tell Darren that these earphones have batteries in them," Rick pleaded. "He doesn't believe me."

Darren, the youngest, sat grinning and shaking his head.

Ken was perplexed. "Son, some earphones have batteries. These don't. These are connected to the stereo."

"No, no," Rick shouted. "They have batteries! I'll bet you!"

Ken says he sighed, believing that all his hard work on teaching the boys wariness had been in vain. "Okay, how much do you want to bet?"

Scott spoke up. "Dad, the odds are definitely in your favor."

Rick hesitated and then responded, "A dollar?"

With sad resignation, Ken opened his wallet and pulled out a dollar. Then he glanced at Darren, who was starting to giggle, and back at Rick, who was fighting back a grin. Scott kept a straight face as Rick walked over to the stereo, raised the earphones and gave them a shake, and two number nine batteries fell to the floor.

"Looks like you lost, Dad," Scott announced, sticking to his role as the shill.

Ken recalls laughing until his sides ached.

Rick asked, "Would you have gone to five?"

Ken just nodded, doubling over with laughter.

In Texas hold 'em parlance, a "Montana banana" describes "hole cards" of nine and two, allegedly because a player's chances of winning with these numbers would be the same as growing bananas in nontropical Montana. With his two number nines, though, Rick had suckered his dad, besting the bettor.

That was the last bet in the Wilson household.

Today, father and sons still engage in games of skill—chess, checkers, hearts, even some friendly poker. Ken is proud that his early training did pay off, producing two Air Force lieutenant colonels and an elementary school teacher. None haunt the casinos.

But, if Ken ever offers to bet his sons, a litany of hilarious questions ensue. Nobody makes a sucker out of Ken's sons. That's his legacy to them.

"You say you will bet us that the sun will rise tomorrow? That's Saturday morning? Right here in this particular state? We'll see it in this sky above us? That's our sun, right, that this planet revolves around?"

Even when it looks like a sure shot, Ken's sons realize that the house edge remains immutable. And merging my life with Ken and his sons proved a best bet for me!

*—Terri Elders*

# You Ain't Doin'
# Nothin' Anyway

Blessed with good health and marked by an active lifestyle, Dad betrayed the aging process for the longest time. He was able to work like a young man well after seventy. Thus, he evaded the normal, gradual decline in physical abilities, only to lose his suddenly and in a very short span of time. This rapid descent was very frustrating for Dad and it contributed to the noticeable increase of impatience he would display from time to time.

Unable to do many of the things he once did, he began to call on me more often for help, with everything from heavy chores to trivial tasks, and his lack of patience compelled him to be very demanding in his requests. Most of the time he just needed an extra pair of hands, and even though we lived only ten miles apart, it wasn't always as convenient for me to respond as he seemed to think it was.

Occasionally, I considered his call for assistance to be impractical and would try to negotiate a more convenient time. But his impatience would not allow him to waver, and he would finally cement his request with, "You ain't doin' nothin', anyway."

Oh, how I hated hearing those words. It's not that Dad was inconsiderate; nothing could be further from the truth. And usually he said it in sort of a half-joking manner. It was just his way of rationalizing his insistent and untimely request. Still, I would cringe every time I heard him say it.

One evening as I was engaged in some yard work, Dad called and wanted me to help him sharpen the blades of his lawnmower. I dickered with him a little while, questioning whether it had to be done right away. He ended our brief discussion with "You ain't doin' nothing anyway."

On another occasion, I had planned to watch a ball game one Saturday afternoon with my son, Casey, who was home from school that weekend. This was a game of keen interest for both Casey and me, and our anticipation grew in the days leading up to it. Dad, however, had other ideas. Just minutes before the game began, the telephone rang and Dad explained that he wanted a ditch dug from the back of the house around to the front to carry the water from one of the downspouts over the hill. And he wanted it done today, right now. I politely resisted as much as possible until I heard, "You ain't doin' nothin' anyway."

I know this sounds a little bizarre, but I seemed to feel a weird sense of gratification when I heard him add, "And bring Casey with you. He ain't doin' nothin' either."

I guess misery truly does love company. These are just two examples of the many times I have been victimized by one of Dad's insistent urges.

About two weeks after the ditch-digging adventure, I took Dad to the emergency room at the hospital. His health was failing him and he looked quite pitiful. He wouldn't admit it, but he was very sick. He knew it, too. Otherwise, he would never have complied with the long wait in the emergency room.

After about three and half hours of waiting, Dad looked up from his watch and said to me, "Boy, I'm going to owe you big time for this."

Somewhat puzzled, I asked, "What do you mean, Dad?"

"Taking up all your time like this," he replied.

Rarely do most of us recognize a special moment as such until later when we look back on it. Occasionally, however, we are granted the liberty to recognize a special moment as it unfolds. This was one of those occasions, and I knew instantly that I had been permitted to partake in something very special.

"Dad," I said. "I wasn't doin' nothin' anyway."

At that moment, a tranquil silence settled upon us as we sat looking into each other's eyes. In his face I saw a man who was thanking me for answering all of his anxious pleas for help. His tired eyes also retold the story of how he had quit school in the sixth grade to work the farm in order to help support the family. As a young boy he hunted with his father to put meat on the table. He picked the corn and dug the potatoes he had planted on the hillside that he plowed behind a mule named Sam.

As a young man, Dad had joined the army and fought for his country on the battlefields of Europe during World War II and then again years later in Vietnam. Except for mentioning some buddies he'd served with, he never spoke of what he'd seen or done.

This is a man who could wield an axe, a hammer, or a crosscut saw with the best of them, and he could build anything from a rabbit hutch to a tobacco barn. Working with his hands was more like recreation for Dad, and it afforded him a great deal of satisfaction.

It was this satisfaction of accomplishment that suddenly became elusive for Dad when age played its dirty trick on him. I now saw that my assistance would, in a small way, ease the pain of having lost what old age had taken from him in such a swift and thoughtless manner.

As I met my father's gaze in the ER that day, I let him know that no thanks were necessary and that my love, respect, and admiration for him—as my father, my mentor, and in many ways my superior—would never allow me to refuse a request from him.

Admittedly, during this turbulent period of my father's life, there were times when I answered some of Dad's untimely requests with a measure of disgruntled submission. And sometimes his requests were not urgent matters requiring the immediate attention he demanded. Regardless of their significance, though, I always responded, and I am so thankful I did.

Dad doesn't call me for help anymore. He recently advanced into the sixth stage of Alzheimer's disease and doesn't even know who I am most of the time. Although he doesn't call anymore, I go and visit with him at every opportunity, and each time I do, I remind myself that, comparatively speaking, I really ain't doin' nothin' anyway.

—*Herbert E. Castle*

# My *Real* Dad

My stepfather didn't have a hair on his chest. That is why I was puzzled by a persistent "body sense" that remained with me, like a shadow, for decades. This "body sense" wasn't an image or a memory; it was palpable, a feeling. My right cheek lay on a chest matted with dark brown hair. It tickled my toddler nose. I felt safe.

I hadn't lived with my real dad since I was four; after that, I'd seen him once, when I was six. His face existed in no family photographs. His figure had faded into a vague description: a dark-haired man not as tall as my stepfather. That was it.

The room is dimly lit, with vivid red walls. A dark wood armoire commands one corner of the room, a glass desk sits directly opposite. I sit on a crème-colored couch, a pillow against the small of my back so my high heels can rest flat on the floor. The cushion beneath me gives gently, and I find the center, which sinks slightly more, the weight of dozens of people before me having broken down the cushion's resistance. My therapist, with black hair cut chin length, silver necklace, and stylish black boots that cause her to tower over me, has guided me to the couch.

I don't know why I tell her about this sense of my right cheek feeling tickled, but she asks me to call it up and to face a black bar. The bar crosses a three-legged tripod that perches on a dark-wooden parson's table, and a pair of cobalt blue lights jet across the bar. She instructs me to track the lights with my eyes for about thirty seconds no matter what images and feelings come up. It is a therapy called Eye Movement Desensitization and Reprocessing, or EMDR, mysterious to me because it de-traumatizes me from the severely violent family life I experienced after my dad was forced to leave, but my memories remain intact. I relate it to REM sleep, in that the eye movement tricks the subconscious into giving up its secrets.

I melt into the sense and I can *feel* the soft curls under my right cheek. And I remember. This man. My dad. My real dad has me tucked inside his arm, scooping my toddler body into him. I am wearing a little pink dress. I am two, and I love to wear dresses. It is nap time, and typically, it is going to take some convincing to get me to slow down and sleep. We are curled on the big bed because I want to be close to him.

So my dad cuddles me, pats my butt, pulls me close, smoothes my baby-fine, straight, brown hair, pulls me close again. I feel safe. I move my head slowly up and down and smile because I feel the hair on his chest so soft and warm. It is a sultry summer day, and there are a few fans but no air conditioning. My dad's skin is a little sticky, but I don't mind. He smells faintly of Brut. He had tossed his sweat-soaked shirt over a dark wooden chair before he lay down with me. He still wears belted trousers, thin dark socks, and brown soft-leather shoes.

He starts singing. Badly. I laugh. He is crooning a made-up lullaby. I sit up, and so does he. Then he bounces me on his lap. We are both laughing.

He pulls me up into his arms, my chubby legs wrapped around his waist, and twirls me around, moving down the hall to the sitting room. I realize there is music. Violin music. My grandfather is playing a concerto; it is cheerful and bouncy. My father and my grandfather are being naughty—they are playing, and we are dancing. Laughter rings through the sunlit mahogany halls of this old Central Park West apartment. Two heavy crystal tumblers—amber liquid pooling beneath semi-melted ice cubes—catch the light, casting rainbows on the walls of the sitting room, where my grandfather usually gives his violin lessons. I hear the traffic noises outside the window—fire trucks screaming, cars beeping, trucks rumbling, normal New York noise that forms a backdrop to everything we do. So, in a way, it is silent.

My grandmother is busy in the other room. I hear her scold gently, calling out, "She's never going to get her nap with you two men being so silly!" Her tone of voice says my grandmother doesn't mind.

My dad spins me and spins me in circles until I am dizzy with laughter . . . all wound up! My grandfather segues his allegretto music into an adagio with luxurious deep tones, and my daddy begins to slow his turns, until he is gently rocking me as he walks me back to the big bed, where he will ease me into sleep, press a kiss onto my forehead, cover me, and tip-toe out of the dark room when he is convinced that sleep has captured me.

I'm nearly falling asleep on the therapist's couch, but the session is over. She turns off the light bar.

My entire body is singing now. There is sparkling energy dancing from my fingers to my toes—every part of me, uniformly.

It is in stark contrast to the physical sense that I usually have when I do EMDR; revisiting the physical and sexual violence perpetrated by my stepfather, my shoulders are often hunched with pain, my head pounding, tears and howls streaming without inhibition, the small of my back tender. Usually, my body slowly releases the pain over the next few days as my mind processes the session.

But not this time. Instead, I am aware of a fine energy pulsing through my entire body that is every bit as joyous as lying in my real dad's arms, my cheek on his furry, warm chest.

This sense of safety and love is recaptured. It is palpable, and it fills me up. The experience I had when I was that little girl enlarges and fills me to become a new reference point for my adult self. I know what I endured two years after that musical interlude. I hear my therapist say that we are reinforcing this furry-chest-on-my-toddler-cheek memory because she wants me to have a good sense to call up, so I will someday again know Love.

This precious, unfamiliar feeling reverberates in me, and I walk out of the tall white door a bit stunned, feeling for the next few minutes like a little kid. But now I know. I know that soft sense on my cheek was a gift, a clue to lead me to recapturing a few moments when I knew I was loved and protected, that nothing and no one could hurt me. Because my daddy was there. For me.

—*Diana Page Jordan*

# Father to Son

The snapshot on the refrigerator tells the whole story. In the photo, my son Joey holds his son Nathaniel. Nathaniel is just under one year old, yet the expression on his face as he looks at his father is one of pure adulation. It says his dad is his source of comfort, fun, and security. Joey is beaming with unmistakable love, pride, and joy. His face and his posture say that this child is the center of his world and he would give his life for him. The picture takes me back to when Joey was Nathaniel's age.

Joseph Nathaniel Walker was born at 9:01 A.M. on December, 17, 1979, weighing in at nine pounds one ounce and screaming heartily. The nurse handed him to me. When I held him close and said, "Hey, Joey," he immediately stopped crying and opened his eyes. The love, pride, and happiness welled up inside me like a volcano ready to blow off the top of a mountain. I had always wanted to be a father, and now, here I was, for better or worse, a dad. I loved that child more than life itself.

When Joey was about a year old, he became ill with a stomach virus and a slight fever. I took him to the doctor, and when they weighed him, I mentioned to the doctor that Joey had lost two pounds. The doctor became concerned and said that, although Joey seemed okay, we had to admit him to the hospital right away and get intravenous fluids into him before he became dehydrated.

I have had an irrational fear of hospitals ever since my own father went into the hospital when I was young. He had lung cancer and never came home. In my mind, people went to the hospital to die, not to get better. So when the doctor told me that we had to put Joey in the hospital, I lost control, crying so hard I could not talk. When I needed to answer a question, all I could do was whimper. Grief and anguish, reborn from my father's death, washed over me like a tidal wave. I could barely breathe. The doctor was shocked and slightly embarrassed by my reaction to what was, in his estimation, a minor procedure. No matter how much he insisted that Joey just had a bug that was not life-threatening, I was inconsolable. The sight of a 6-foot, 3-inch, 250-pound man blubbering like a baby over something that was serious but certainly not deadly must have been disconcerting.

After a while, I regained enough composure to call my wife, Andrea, to tell her what was going on, but then I started crying again before I could finish. All this emotion from a Navy veteran and firefighter who had seen death up close and personal, who had pulled people out of burning buildings and ocean waters, performed CPR and emergency first aid, was, at the least, very embarrassing. Though upset and concerned, Andrea was like a rock, steady and strong enough for me to lean on.

Joey spent three days in the hospital with one of us at his side every minute. Of course, he recovered and grew up to be a happy and healthy boy. But those were three long days, and I'll never forget how the very thought of serious harm coming to my precious son had devastated me.

Twenty-five years later, Joey called one evening two weeks before Nathaniel's first birthday.

"Dad—" he said, then stopped, struggling to suppress his emotions.

"Joey," I said, "What's wrong?"

"Dad—" he choked out again.

"Joey," I said, my voice rising with alarm, "what is it?"

"We're at the hospital with Nathaniel."

Choking back my own fear, I again asked, "What is it?"

"Nathaniel has holes in his skull," Joey cried. "He's got some kind of disease that's eating holes in his skull."

I sat dumbfounded, unable to speak, for a few seconds. Finally, I asked, "What is this disease called?"

"I don't know," he sobbed. "All I know is that my son has freaking holes in his skull."

"Look, the Children's Hospital in Atlanta is one of the best in the world, with top-notch doctors. Nathaniel's in good hands. This is going to be alright," I said, hoping I sounded more confident than I felt. "We will drive up there first thing in the morning."

After we hung up, I searched the Internet for information on diseases that cause holes to form in a child's skull, but Joey had been so vague that it was useless. Andrea e-mailed Joey's mother-in-law, asking if she had any more information. Then we went to bed.

When Andrea was asleep, I got down on my knees and cried while I prayed to God, "Please, do not take my precious grandson away from my son."

We woke up after a few brief hours of sleep. While I made coffee and packed, Andrea checked her e-mail. Joey's mother-in-law had replied that Nathaniel was being referred to oncology. Distraught, we made the normally five-hour trip to Atlanta from Pensacola in a little over four hours. We met Joey and his wife, Hollis, at the hospital.

When Joey and I embraced and reassured each other, our common bond was forged, a bond men share in their unconditional love for their sons. This love knows no boundaries or compromises; it is a love that lasts forever, no matter what. The bond I had missed sharing with my own father.

As we waited in the hospital family room and I watched Joey, I sensed that we also shared an almost primal urge, a need, to smash and destroy anything that threatens our children. However, once I realized all my strength and rage are toothless against microbes and cells that attack from within, the feeling of powerlessness became as emotionally and physically draining as a marathon run.

After four days of extensive testing, Nathaniel was diagnosed with Langerhans cell histiocytosis, a disease that attacks healthy tissue, including the blood, bone, skin, and liver. Although it is not a cancer, chemotherapy is the prescribed treatment. LCH is rarely fatal, and children often outgrow it while being treated, but patients often need a liver transplant later in life.

Nathaniel endured a year and a half of various chemotherapy treatments, but he is now fully recovered, happy, and healthy. He loves cars and trucks, books and blocks, and fusses when his mom tries to wipe his face. He's growing, and his appetite is making up for lost time.

About a year after Nathaniel's diagnosis, I was in the kitchen, ostensibly to clean but actually getting a snack, while waiting for the kids to arrive from Atlanta. Joey had just called to say they were still an hour and a half away. As I prepared my snack, I heard the door open. When I turned, I saw Nathaniel standing there holding a stuffed bear.

"Hey, Grandpa," Nathaniel said smiling.

I ran to him, hugged and kissed him, saying, "Hey, baby boy!"

Joey and Hollis came in laughing. "We fooled you."

"Yeah, you got me, but I got the best laugh. You're here!"

That night after everyone had gone to bed, Joey and I shared some wayward "It's a Boy" cigars he had found at home. We talked about life and love. I mentioned that now that he had a son of his own, he knew just how much he himself had been loved.

"I have always known," he said.

"I've heard that a man does not know the true meaning of love until he holds his first child."

"Well, Pops," Joey said, "I can't disagree with that."

—*Bob Walker*

# Sorry, Dad

When my age was still in the single digits, I was Daddy's little girl. We were pals.

My parents divorced when I was ten. My siblings were seven, eight, and nine years older than me, so when the family fractured, my father went from being a husband with a family of six to a single dad with a teenager of one.

And oh, what a teenager I was!

Having grown up in a large family and then creating a large family of his own, Dad was used to having options when infractions were committed. If Dad found something amiss, he would say in his best commander of a military post voice, "Whooo left the cap off the shampoo?" "Whooo left the back door open?" "Whooo left the milk in the living room?"

When there were six of us in the house, no one ever confessed to it. So, even as a small child, I wondered why he bothered. When it became just the two of us in the house, his commander-style whooo-did-it served as the perfect launch vehicle for my teenaged angst. Whenever he would ask one of his famous "whooo" questions, I would roll my eyes and ask him, with as much sarcasm as my teenage soul could generate, "Now, Daaad, there's only two of us who live here. If you know it wasn't *you*, that doesn't leave many options, now, does it?"

Instead of shoving my swelled head into the toilet and giving me 2,000 flushes, which I deserved, Dad would issue a few frustrated mumbles and deep-trenched scowls as he retreated into the safety of his room, away from this foreign person who had come to live in his house.

Gone was Daddy's little girl. Instead, my father found himself to be the chief cook and bottle washer for a belligerent teen with a cup of attitude and a side dish of fury. There weren't enough whips and chairs to keep that lion at bay. No matter how harshly I lashed out, Dad never fought back. He simply retreated and gave me more space.

In my search for an adversary upon whom to vent my fury, I decided to up the ante. I would do for anything to be defiant. When Dad asked me to sweep the kitchen floor, I did. Then I would take the dust pan full of dust, crumbs, and kitchen shrapnel and dump it into his work boots. I remember sitting at the kitchen table pretending to eat my breakfast the next morning and waiting for Dad to notice what I had done. He did not pause, did not dump his boots out, did not even raise his eyes to look at me. He just put on his boots and went to work. If I did it once, I must have done it a hundred times, and not once did Dad comment on the debris accumulating inside his highly polished black work boots.

One afternoon, Dad came home and asked, "Whooo left the cap off the shampoo?"

To which I heard myself answer, "Amy did it." I have no idea where it came from; it just fell out of my smarmy little mouth.

"Amy did it," became my automatic reply to all of Dad's "whooo" questions.

After many weeks, Dad finally asked me, "Who is this Amy? Is she some new friend of yours?"

"She's a ghost, Dad," I told him straight-faced. "She lives in the cold room in the basement. She was murdered in this house, and she can't leave until I figure out who killed her."

Dad went to his room.

I didn't believe in Amy, but it got a reaction out of Dad, so I hung on to it like a sixteen-year-old boy to the keys of his new sports car. For months I tormented my father with Amy stories.

"Dad, can we turn up the heat? Amy's cold."

"Dad, where do they keep the records of the dead?"

"Dad, how long would it take to dig up the basement?"

The only responses I ever got were "humph" and a few raised eyebrows.

For my next teenage trick, I decided to miss the bus and force Dad to drive me to school. I succeeded in missing the bus by refusing to get up when he called me. In this particular battle of wills, Dad, ever refusing to raise his voice at me, decided he's just pull the blankets off my bed and put them on the floor in the living room. This small move did give him the upper hand for a few days.

Then, ever evil, I went into the basement, got one of the sleeping bags down, unrolled it, and tied it by its strings to the head of my bed.

The next morning, I shuddered with unspoken giggles as Dad began the dance of calling me to get up. After the third unsuccessful try, he opened my door, grabbed the bottom of the blanket, and gave it a yank. Instead of it whisking dramatically off the bed, Dad ended up pitching forward and cracking his head on my footboard.

I don't remember if I even went to school that day. I just remember my personal sense of victory. I had won another round, or at least felt I had.

A few days later, a new radio/alarm clock appeared on the kitchen table. I assumed it was for Dad, but it was really nice and fancy-looking, so I swiped it and put it in my room. (Like he didn't have that planned.) After that, I got to get myself up.

We had a great game of "button-button," in which I'd move his toothbrush around the bathroom, putting it in different drawers, forcing him to hunt for it a couple of mornings a week. I used to write my name in the toilet with his shaving cream so he'd run out faster.

Memory is funny. I remember exactly when each of our wars began, but I don't remember when any of them ended.

They did end. By the time I got through high school, we were friends again, and now, even though I outweigh him by about thirty pounds, I am once again Daddy's little girl. I love my dad.

A few years ago, he and his new wife came to my house for Dad's birthday supper. I undeservedly have a husband and two kind and gentle children. It was all very nice. It was great. We had supper, cake, presents, and cards.

When Dad opened the card from my husband and me, he read it, sat silently for a moment, then leaned toward me across the table and scowled.

"Think you're funny, don't you," he said.

I had signed it, "Love from Dave, Allison, and Amy."

I had to laugh. I rocked in my chair I laughed so hard. Finally, I regained my decorum and said, "Sorry, Dad."

Dad nodded his head at me and said, "Me, too."

I didn't get it right away. I didn't get it until after I had gone to bed that night. My father thought he had made mistakes. He thought, somehow, that he had failed me either with the divorce or during our warring years.

Looking back, I think he did it all just right. It's hard to have a war all by yourself. Instead of picking up the sword and fighting back, Dad just accepted all his stab wounds until my arm got tired and I quit.

Again, and for the record, "Sorry, Dad . . . And, um, thanks."

*—Allison Maher*

# Ya Gotta Put a
# Lotta Love into It

My father and I have always seen things differently. He is a self-made entrepreneur who has always viewed the ideal life as one that included having a stable career, owning a comfortable home, and driving a fine-tuned automobile. He has always valued family, planning ahead, and investing for the future.

I, however, saw a rather different picture—one that included me traveling across numerous countries, holding myriad jobs, and writing about my experiences from various apartments or hotel rooms. I have always been a fly-by-the-seat-of-my-pants kind of gal.

That is why one summer when I announced I was going to take a long road trip across the American West, Dad frowned and told me it was a bad idea. And it is why a few years later, when I ventured to Arizona for a yoga-teacher training program, he labeled my endeavor as "risky and unnecessary." Since I lived in such close proximity to New York City, he reasoned, surely there were yoga studios nearby; why did I need to travel so far by myself?

Yes, my father and I surely have had our share of disparities. Our idea of the perfect meal is no exception. To me, a vegetarian, the perfect meal consists of tofu lasagna coupled with a big salad. My father, on the other hand, prefers a thick, tender steak paired with gravy and more thick, tender steak.

So, recently, when Father's Day was approaching and my sisters elected me in charge of planning a dinner in honor of our dad, I was a little worried. Most of the restaurants I frequented were either vegan or Japanese. Since my father is a carnivore who has an aversion to eating with chopsticks, both of these venues were completely out of the question. After a few hours of research on the Internet, however, I found a suitable place. Though I cringed at the thought, I made reservations at the best steakhouse in the area. Even though sitting in a "house of steak" was a bit out of my comfort zone, I figured it was a small price to pay to make my father happy.

When the day arrived, I drove to my parents' house dressed in my Sunday best, ready to go to the restaurant. I found my father strolling around the backyard and tending to the koi pond and adjacent garden, which he built with his own hands. Once inside the house, I noticed no one was getting ready for our early dinner at the restaurant. My two sisters were nowhere to be found, and my mother, who was perusing a magazine at the kitchen table, greeted me with a nearly somber expression.

"I don't think he wants to go to the restaurant," she informed me. "So why don't you go talk to him?"

I went outside to the yard, where my father verified my mother's assumption. He said he did not want to spend the day at the steakhouse and would rather just have a barbecue here. So it was settled. But the afternoon was slipping away, and I was still in charge of the day's events. And we needed food. Promptly, I made a list. Then, I rounded up my sister for a quick trip to the local grocery store.

We spent a total of eighty dollars on rib eye, shrimp, vegetables, fixings, and dessert. Since there was no time to properly marinate the steaks, I prepared a quick, savory rub of dried herbs and fresh garlic. As I did so, I was reminded of my grandmother, who is known for her out-of-this-world lasagna. When asked for the secret of this gastronomical delight, she simply said, "Love. You gotta put a lotta love in it."

With this in mind, I rubbed down those steaks with love in my heart, in spite of the fact I would not be eating them, and then seasoned the veggies, which I would be eating in abundance, for the grill. Meanwhile, my mother prepared a big green salad and my sisters set the table with brightly colored paper plates and flowered napkins. While all this was underway, my father intermittently sat on the patio and took quick dips in the pool.

In less than two hours, our work was done. We brought the tray of herbed steaks and vegetables to our father, who fired up the grill and, of course, cooked everything to perfection. At the dinner table, everyone complimented me on the success of the day.

As I caught glimpses of my father taking extra helpings of grilled vegetables and salad, I began to think that perhaps we were not so dissimilar, after all.

My mind drifted back to our differences of the past. Of course, in a way he was right about my cross-country trip, because I ran out of money a week before my return home. But upon my arrival, instead of lecturing me about my oversight or saying, "I told you so," he shared in my joy as I showed him hundreds of pictures of my amazing adventures at sites like the Black Hills of South Dakota, Yellowstone National Park, and Montana's Gallatin River. What's more, since I have become a yoga instructor, he has consulted me plenty of times to help him stretch his aching back.

Technically speaking, my dad cooked his own Father's Day dinner. However, he was not crammed in the tiny lobby and then at a crowded table of a popular restaurant on one of its busiest days of the season. Instead, my father spent the afternoon at his leisure, under the warm June sunshine, togged up in bathing shorts and flip flops rather than a starched shirt.

Later the following evening, I was at home, unwinding with a book, when the phone rang. I was caught off guard when I heard my father's voice on the other end. This is because my mother is the one who usually calls me.

Apprehensively, I spoke. "Hi, Dad. Is everything okay?"

"Yeah, everything's fine." His voice was relaxed and cheery.

I, however, was still a little puzzled as to the reason for his call and waited for an explanation.

"I was calling to say thanks for a wonderful Father's Day."

"Sure, Dad," I replied, "I'm glad you liked it."

"I can't remember the last time I've had such a nice day," he said.

Now that I think of it, neither can I.

—*Melissa Gentile*

# Sweeping Effects

I t was the sweeping that really counted when I was a child. Vexed to the breaking point by my lackadaisical efforts, my father more than once gently took the broom from my small freckled hand and showed me how to reach more deeply into the corner, farther under the table, more assiduously into the crack between the door and the outside. Watching him sweep the dust and detritus into a neat pile on our fifties-era red-speckled linoleum floor, I was certain that no one had a better dad. He could do everything and do it the best way. Even his method of scooping up the linty pile was a demonstration of his cleverness. My dad used an old newspaper or the edge of a piece of cardboard to pick up the collected dust. He taught me exactly how. As I grew older, I saw other people had dustpans in their homes. Steel ones, plastic ones, color coordinated with their kitchens, hanging in the utility closet. It was clear that these people were softies, ne'er-do-wells, mildly degenerate, obviously not as resourceful as my dad.

On a recent Father's Day I got my dad a broom at Costco—black, slanty nylon bristles, long shiny yellow handle, ready for action. I didn't go so far as to get him a dustpan; I knew better. Even with the new shirts from my brothers and a biking tool from my sister, I knew it was his favorite gift. For his seventy-eighth birthday, I went all out and got him a Swiffer. This was a newfangled sweeper, so it was a risk. But you should have seen his eyes light up.

During my childhood, my father was the heavy and got the blame for the big arguments. Now, as a single mom, I know that some arguments need to happen and that someone has to start them. And now I wish there were someone else around to start them with my own kids, someone besides me to be the heavy. My father demanded that we clean our own messes, straighten our rooms, clean our assigned bathroom, take out the trash, and, of course, sweep. These days at my house, when I am faced with one recalcitrant teenager glued to a computer game, another crashing action figures into the bathtub instead of scrubbing it, and the third writing from college for money, it might be nice for someone other than me to fight the parental battles.

My father's steadfast kindness and loyal presence constantly reminds me of what my children don't have. Their father lives three thousand miles away and is not center stage in their lives.

When I brag about their grandfather, I am afraid it will remind my children of what they are missing. But maybe they don't think that way because what they are missing has simply become their real life. It seems redundant to say that you don't see what is invisible to you. I pretend that they can't see fathers in other people's lives. If we walk quickly enough, stay busy enough, maybe they won't notice the dad throwing a softball to his son in the park or the one hugging his daughter in a restaurant.

When the kids and I moved last year, my father spent all day lugging furniture and breaking down boxes while my mom and I were unpacking.

When I couldn't take one more push on a phantom brake pedal as my two sons were learning to drive, my father risked life and limb to teach them on city streets in his own car. His stained-glass lamps adorn two of the rooms in my house; his pottery is in my cupboards.

Last week my dad came over and recruited my seventeen-year-old son to help him fix our backyard gate, which had been hanging askew for months. They worked for hours on the heavy wooden monolith, exhuming the electric screwdriver, replacing a board, balancing the hinges. My father will be eighty-four next year. He has been my rock for every minute of every day that I have been here.

There are not many society pages that extol the virtues of fatherhood. Not many top-forty songs written about dads being there raising children. Not many cutting-edge articles in *Gentleman's Quarterly* about hardworking dads looking suave at Chuck E. Cheese. Father's Day at my parents' house is always half of what Mother's Day is. I am pretty sure my father doesn't care. He has never longed for acknowledgement, never chided us for forgetting his birthday or anniversary. He is embarrassed by presents and compliments.

Contrary to what popular culture and political pundits extol, having my father in my life has shown me that one parent is not an ideal number for raising children, even though, in my children's case, it has had to be. I can only imagine that, if all fathers really understood that they are the biggest celebrities in their children's world, for every day of their lives, more dads would stay and bask in the glory of that unstinting admiration. It would be unthinkable, ridiculous, to abandon or neglect their fan base. How do I know? Because I am still compelled to defend my children's father in order to allow them some semblance of that imagined hero in their lives. Because I can't bear the thought that I have something they don't.

I'd like to think my father stuck around because his kids were so endearing and easy to raise. But that thought would have made even Mother Teresa (had she known us) run screaming in hysterical laughter down the streets of Calcutta. We were not easy. My father was just stalwart.

I have been loved, cared for, taught, and disciplined by two parents who, together, have, ironically, made me whole enough to be able to raise three children without their own dad.

And so I know from all angles that a father has a sweeping effect on the lives of his children—whether with brooms or birthdays or simply showing up.

—*Jolie Kanat*

# What Fathers Do

My father can't explain the rationale of calculus or the activities on Wall Street. He doesn't understand a thing about computers; wouldn't know a motherboard from a washboard. A father of the fifties and sixties, he doesn't cook, do laundry, make beds, or iron clothes. I doubt he ever changed a diaper in his life. But whatever Daddy lacks in technological proficiency and domestic skills, he has made up for in other ways.

As a child, I thought of my father as a brave man. A man who always made things better.

In my first recollection of him, I am a toddler. He is holding me in his arms, walking me around a dimly lit room while I cry, frightened by a nightmare. My breath comes out in jerky gasps, and even now, I can still hear Daddy's smooth baritone voice as he softly prays for his scared little girl.

When I was six, I attempted to show off my bike-riding skills to an important guest. Instead of the flawless demonstration I had hoped for, I was mortified when I crashed headlong into the side of the house, nearly breaking my neck in the process. My father tenderly led me into the house for some first aid, both to my skinned knees and my wounded pride.

Daddy often drove me and my sisters to the library after school, where he would wait patiently while we checked out mountains of books. One afternoon, while racing to the car, I tripped over a large crack in the sidewalk and flew through the air, landing with a brutal bang on hands and knees, books scattering in every direction. As I looked up, still too stunned to cry, I saw Daddy leap out of the car and race to my side. After inspecting my scrapes, he scooped me up and carried me to the car. How safe I felt in his arms.

There is an old picture somewhere of my dad holding up a dead snake as long as he is tall. As a little girl, I used to stare at that picture and think, *How could anybody be so brave?*

But that is what good fathers do. They kill the snakes. They do what nobody else wants to do.

If we had a flat tire, Daddy got out in the heat or rain or sleet and changed it.

If a noise woke us in the night, Daddy was expected to go check it out.

If we got caught in a rainstorm while driving to church or out to eat, it was understood that Daddy would let us out at the door, go park the car alone, and get drenched on his way inside.

If the roof leaked, we never doubted that Daddy would find the hole and plug it.

If a mouse left evidence lying around, Daddy was expected to bait a trap, inspect it for success, and dispose of whatever landed there.

And at the end of the day, Daddy was the one who sat at a little scuffed desk and paid the bills. Not once do I recall him mentioning money being tight, even though I feel certain there were times when it was.

My dad was the proverbial knight in shining armor in my young eyes. As the years passed, though, I came to the shocking realization that fathers aren't perfect—not even those who kill snakes. They make mistakes. They act like jerks. And sometimes they break their children's hearts.

But I also learned that, whenever fathers acknowledge their mistakes, mend their ways, and ask their children to forgive them, they are brave indeed.

Eventually, I got too big and too proud for my dad to carry me around after a bad fall, but he still carried me in his heart.

At twenty-two, I became engaged to a handsome young man with eyes the color of a robin's egg. James was going to make my every dream come true. We planned a late-summer wedding; I couldn't wait for my father to escort me down the aisle.

Then one night, three weeks before the wedding, James called to say it was off. Just like that. No face-to-face conversation. Just a meager phone call. Oh, he offered his reasons, but they sounded like a foreign language to me; I couldn't understand a word he said. I only knew that my heart ached. It felt like a giant stone sat on my chest. Not only was my heart broken, but I anguished over all the planning and the purchases, including my wedding gown and the four hundred invitations that were to be mailed the very next day. I thought of all the gifts that friends and relatives had already sent that would now have to be returned with a sad note attached: "Thank you for your generous gift of such and so, but I regret to inform you that the wedding has been cancelled." Deep down, I wanted to die.

The next morning, James called saying he needed to see me in person before leaving town.

When he knocked on the door, I moved to open it, but my father beat me to it.

In one swift motion, Daddy opened the door and said, "Now, James, I want you to know that I'm not pleased that you've broken Dayle's heart. You need to say whatever you came to say to her, then leave immediately. Is that understood?"

My father is a tall man, and he'd never looked taller to me—nor James more terrified. I honestly thought Daddy might punch him.

As Sigmund Freud once said, "I cannot think of any need in childhood as strong as the need for a father's protection."

And I don't think you fully outgrow that need. Even though I have a wonderful husband and a grown daughter now, it comforts me to know that, should I ever encounter a real crisis in my life, my dad, on a moment's notice, would drive the distance to make it better. He would kill the snake, dispose of the remains, and hug my fear away. He is, after all, my father, and that is what fathers do.

—*Dayle Allen Shockley*

# Three Precious Words

The shadow of a ginkgo tree danced in the apartment window as I lay snuggled up in bed about to turn out the light. I was growing agitated. My night-owl husband still hadn't come to bed. I heard the faint sound of the phone ring. Then whispers.

I walked into the darkened living room and heard my husband Kelvin say, "What's going on?" as he clicked on the table lamp. He listened for a while and handed me the phone.

The news on the phone wasn't good. My dad had suffered a major heart attack while he was jogging on his treadmill. In a few days, he was going into surgery for a quintuple bypass.

"The doctor said he was lucky he'd come in when he had. They were able to stop the heart attack with medication," explained my mom, trying to sound calm.

When I hung up the phone, I felt numb and dizzy. I couldn't believe this was happening. Two months earlier we had moved our family to my husband's new duty station at Osan Air Force base in South Korea.

"Why now?" I said to my husband.

He wrapped his arms around me, trying to comfort me, but no comfort came. He made a pot of decaf and poured me a cup as we sat at the kitchen table. The coffee tasted bitter, and I poured it down the sink.

"I'm sorry," I told him, not wanting to hurt his feelings. But he knew it wasn't his coffee.

I couldn't sleep that night as worry further tightened its grip. I felt nauseous and found it hard to breathe. Still awake and exhausted at 3:00 A.M., I could no longer fight back tears.

The next day, the few friends I'd made on base tried to rally around me, asking if I wanted to hang out to get my mind off things. They wanted to take me shopping downtown for Korean pottery and to a favorite Korean restaurant for a lunch of beef bulgogi, sticky rice, and cucumber kimchi.

I declined, wanting only to be with my husband and sons. I was afraid my tightly wound, put-together self would unravel abruptly in front of them, leaving me fully exposed. I didn't know them well enough.

Our family went to the Burger King on base, but I couldn't eat. I watched my boys happily climb the indoor play fort, giggling as they slid down the slide one behind the other. My two-year-old, Colby, pulled off his dingy socks and threw them on the floor. His big brother, Cameron, kept running back to the table to grab fries. They had no idea their grandfather was so sick.

My husband reached across the table and grabbed my hand. "I love you, sweet," he said.

I bit my lip and brushed a tear from my cheek. At that moment, I realized that I'd never heard those words from my father.

My dad came from a family that never said "I love you." My mom spoke those words to us often. But I don't remember Dad ever saying it to me or my brother, although there was never a time that I didn't *feel* loved by him.

My mom worked during the summers, and Dad spent time with us in the afternoons because he often worked the night shift. He'd take us to the movies, McDonald's, the park. During the school year, he'd even come along on field trips.

Most of the time, I was proud he was my dad. Although my father never wore black socks with shorts like some dads do, he did find pleasure in embarrassing me. Growing up, he'd make silly comments to waitresses at restaurants, and I'd want to crawl under the table and not come out. Or he'd share humiliating things about me with my high school friends. With my dates, he'd put on a mean face and scare them with big talk of his shotgun and his prior Marine Corps service—then laugh about it later. Even after I was married, his sense of humor never faded. He continued to share his latest corny joke with me and everyone around. Dad has never been the type to talk about anything serious.

Instead of jokes, what I've really wanted was to hear those three precious words. My husband advised me to say the words first, to tell my dad I loved him. But I wasn't sure I could do it; I was afraid. How would he respond? Would he say those three precious words I longed to hear?

I wanted to catch a plane as fast as possible to get home to my family—to see my father one more time, just in case. But when I spoke to Dad on the phone about it, his heart rate skyrocketed. I heard slow steady beeps become rapid and short. He told me to stay put.

"I'd be worried about you flying," he said as he gasped for air.

Mom got on the phone and said the same. Dad finally calmed down. His heart rate returned to normal. I reluctantly stayed in Korea.

I called him a few hours before his surgery. His voice sounded shaky. I knew he was scared. So was I.

I took a deep breath and swallowed hard. Then I finally said it. "I love you, Dad."

He started to cry. Pretty soon, we were both sobbing. He couldn't talk, so he handed the phone to my mother.

"It's going to be okay," she whispered, choking back her own tears.

My dad made it through the surgery that day, and he's healthier than ever. He's lost a lot of weight. I almost didn't recognize him when I got off the plane when we returned to the states nearly a year later. He stood there next to Mom with a huge smile on his face as we rushed over to them.

God had given me another chance. This time, I could say it in person. But before I could get the words out, Dad hugged me more tightly than he ever had.

"I love you," he whispered.

Then, he told Cameron and Colby he loved them, too.

From that day forward, Dad has been the first to say those three precious words every time.

—*Kim Rogers*

# Love and Money

In the top dresser drawer where my father kept his socks and underwear, he also kept an envelope of money. A white letter-sized envelope, not sealed, not folded, not hidden. In fact, to reach into the envelope you needed only to open the drawer a few inches, and there it was right in front—an envelope of money held in place by a pile of underwear, a necessity among necessities.

The envelope never held much money. Some singles, a few fives, a couple of tens; I don't ever recall finding a twenty or anything larger. On the other hand, I don't ever recall finding the envelope empty.

It took some years for me to realize that this whole business of having an automatically replenishing envelope of money was unusual. My friends got an allowance. The difference between the envelope and the allowance was clear if one of my friends

(Johnny Belbin leaps to mind) came up a few cents short during a Saturday afternoon trip to McDonald's or Burger King or Kentucky Fried Chicken or Chicken Delight or Arby's or the Pancake House or Tom's Grill or the Fish Keg, or we could forget the meal altogether and go right to Dairy Queen for double-dipped cones or hot fudge brownie delights. And these were just the choices within walking distance. The point is that these ritual out-for-lunch excursions were central to my childhood, and by the time I was nine or ten years old, I fully appreciated a basic fact of life: you need money to eat. What I didn't fully appreciate is where that money came from. How did that automatically replenishing envelope really work?

My dad was never one for fatherly lectures or long-winded explanations. He preferred funny stories, jokes, something with a clever closing line. Around this money-envelope business, he and I had a little routine in which I'd say, "Dad, I took some money today from the envelope, but I didn't spend it all. Do you want the change?" He would put his hands on his slim hips, shake his head, and say, "No, keep the change. Invest it wisely in real estate."

That is exactly what he did . . . invest wisely in real estate. Metropolitan Structures, where he worked for over thirty years, built, managed, and/or financed massive commercial developments in Chicago, Baltimore, Boston, Houston, Los Angeles, and Montreal. My dad's successful career was no doubt a source of great vitality and joy and pride for him—a genuine triumph, especially for someone who, right up to his dying days, could easily drink a fifth of whiskey a day.

This can't be glossed over: my dad was an alcoholic. Some family members prefer to say he just had "an unusual relationship with alcohol." Fine. But throughout my childhood, there was always a bottle by my dad's side of the bed, and many nights I watched him sit on the edge of the mattress and take a few gulps before lying down and then, in the morning, a few gulps before standing up. There was also a bottle in his desk drawer at work, and I still remember how, when he came home in the evening, I would eagerly climb onto the kitchen counter to reach the bottle in the cabinet. As the youngest of four sons, it was a big day when I could read the label myself—Johnny Walker—and pour a nice full glass (was it eight ounces?) without spilling, leaving just enough room for two cubes of ice.

An alcoholic, yes. But my dad never (almost never) became sloppy drunk and was truly never—absolutely never—abusive in any way at all. So one way to understand the drinking is to say that it simply helped him deal with life. It helped him function, helped him stay calm and cheerful and focused on what mattered to him most: the envelope held in place by the underwear.

My dad grew up in the poverty familiar to so many first-generation American Jews, and this central fact of his life is captured by one particular story. It's the 1930s, the middle of the night, and my dad, about ten years old, is woken up from a deep sleep and told to be quiet and to pack his things quickly in the darkness because the family is moving to another apartment. Yet another apartment. Every couple months, there was yet another apartment. They would move in the middle of the night— taking their old clawfoot bathtub with them— because they hadn't paid the rent.

Given this childhood trauma, it is little wonder my dad ended up in the real estate business and that my family had the same Evanston, Illinois, address for thirty-two years. But before achieving his rock-solid steadiness, my dad had some pretty rough-and-tumble times. He wasn't just a drinker—he was a fighter too.

For example, although he never saw combat because of a medical discharge, he volunteered for the paratroopers because he thought it would give him the best opportunity, as he once put it, "to go to Germany and kill Nazis." Apparently, he was particularly handy with a gun, so when he got out of the army, he took a job managing a South Side Chicago hotel with the upscale name "The Bennington." It served mostly people who had just been released from jail. As hotel manager, my dad wore a gun on his hip, another in an ankle holster, and carried a sawed-off shotgun when he went back and forth from the hotel to the car.

In our own house, there was only one time when my dad took out a gun—when my Aunt Charlotte, who suffered from schizophrenia, brought home a man who was drinking and shouting and keeping the kids awake. As the story goes, when he was told to leave, the guy broke a bottle and came at my dad with the jagged edge. All of this occurred before I was born, but I remember my dad telling the story with this particular coda: "You never take out a gun unless you're ready to use it, and you never use it unless you're ready to take a man's life."

No surprise—that fella left the house.

It's also no surprise that my dad took the police exam and considered a career with the Chicago police department. He would have been a good cop, I'm sure, and though he had only a twelfth-grade education, I like to think he would have successfully climbed the ranks. Lieutenant? Captain? Police Commissioner? Who knows.

My dad did climb to the position of general partner with Metropolitan Structures, which eventually became affiliated with Metropolitan Life Insurance. By the late 1960s, when I was a little boy, all of the guns were gone and my dad had a fancy office on a high floor in the Illinois Center One building on Wacker Drive, with a view from his large picture window of Michigan Avenue and the Wrigley Building and the mighty Chicago River famously flowing backward away from the Great Lake. It was magical—all of it, the river, the view, the office, the whole Oz-like world of money, power, and success.

I once asked my dad how to respond when other kids asked me, "What does your dad do for a living?"

He answered without a moment's hesitation. "Business," he said. "Tell them that your dad is a businessman."

So I told them. But I could only admire my dad-the-businessman from afar . . . until I was in my mid-thirties and, through an incredible series of coincidences, I landed a freelance writing job working for a New York communications firm hired by an Australian conglomerate that happened to be buying 56 billion dollars worth of U.S. real estate assets. The result was that I spent two days in Chicago interviewing people my dad had worked with for twenty-five years. Some of these Chicago businessmen made the connection right away, and as soon as they realized they were being interviewed by Ben Levis's son, they couldn't answer my questions thoroughly enough and practically took me home with them for dinner. Others never made the connection, and I never said anything. My dad wasn't one to drop names, so it didn't seem right for me to drop his.

But there was one time when I couldn't resist name-dropping, couldn't help pointing out that I was somehow special because I was Ben Levis's son.

To appreciate this incident, you need to understand that as a hungry freelance writer in New York I had accepted this assignment without knowing anything about the real estate business. For the first few weeks, it was great fun calling my dad from hotels in Dallas or San Francisco or Boston or L.A., and telling him that I'd had another full day of interviews with various real estate hotshots in which I'd asked questions and taken notes and now I needed to please know what the hell all this means. My dad would patiently explain the business jargon and prep me for the next set of interviews, until, finally, it was time for the Chicago trip.

It turns out that one of the people I was going to interview was someone my dad knew well but didn't particularly like. A "momzer," he called him, a "shmegege," a "putz."

When it came time for the interview, sure enough, the man was pompous and abrasive, and I was, at least initially, grateful that he failed to make the connection between me and my father.

But then, as I was leaving his office, the guy said in a self-important, patronizing tone of voice, "Well, young man, you seem to know a great deal about all of this—the proliferation of real estate investment trusts, the recent trend toward securitization, the broader implications for the financial services industry. Where did you go to business school?"

It was a delicious moment. I remember taking my time as I said to this momzer, this shmegege, this putz, "I didn't go to business school, but my dad is Ben Levis."

And so it goes that I will always be grateful for the chance I had to appreciate my father's world, his work, that which made possible the automatically replenishing envelope of money. And I think I finally understand—now, today—the secret to that envelope. It has to do with something so obvious to me right this minute that I could kick myself for not getting it before. It's right there in the strange overlap between the language of money and the language of love: the way we talk about interest and securities and trusts and bonds.

And we know that money is somehow tender.

I never had a chance to talk with my dad about this overlap of language. Some insights, I guess, just come too late. But if he could hear me now, I would tell him: "I get it, Dad. I see how that envelope business really worked. It wasn't filled with money. It was filled with your interest, your trust, your bond. There was, in fact, nothing in that envelope at all but your love—a love that was never, never, never withheld. And now—well, now, Dad, it's time to say goodbye. I know how you always appreciated a good closing line, so I want to leave you with this one, by Thornton Wilder: 'There is a land of the living and a land of the dead, and the bridge is love, the only survivor, the only meaning.'"

—*Walter B. Levis*

# DIY

Measure twice and cut once. The carpenter's motto has always been one of my father's favorite sayings, and it certainly applies to life as well as to wood. But it did not seem to be working very well for the old walls of my house that bulged here and leaned there.

Eyeing the unrepentant slab of dust-covered drywall with frustration, I began the messy, laborious job of shaving off the quarter of an inch that kept it from fitting properly. White dust and blue rhetoric clouded the air by the time it finally fit into place and I could start to apply the seam tape and the thick, messy coat of plaster. When the phone rang, I was as coated in plaster as the wall and my hand stuck nicely to the receiver when I picked it up.

"Hi, how's it going?" my sister's cheery voice answered my snarling "Hello." "I just called to check up on you and see what sort of construction or destruction you were doing," she said as a glob of plaster dripped from the telephone and slid down my neck.

I looked from the plaster-coated phone to the dust-filled room. "Have you invested in some sort of crystal ball?" I asked.

I had not spoken to Tanya for a few weeks and, even though our family grapevine works with the speed of light, I was surprised by her question.

"No, but I just talked to Mike, and he is tearing out someone's basement. And yesterday Debbie called to say they were going to start clearing the land for their new house today. And Dad and I are redoing the plumbing in the downstairs bathroom. We just discovered that we have hooked the hot water to the toilet by mistake. Gives a whole new meaning to the saying, 'I'm having a hot flush.' I am sure it would be great in the winter, but we probably should fix that. Now we have to find out where we crossed the pipes when we snaked them through the wall," she explained. "So with all of us in DIY mode, I thought I'd give you a call while we took a break and see what mess you're in."

Mom and Dad were visiting my sister. It made sense that Dad would be helping her with renovations to her two-hundred-year-old home. I looked at my mud-encrusted hands and grinned. At least my walls did not have built-in heating.

It always astonishes me when someone says that they can't hang a picture or screw in a light bulb. In our family, if you want work done on your house you simply do it yourself. All it takes is for someone to say, "It would be nice if there were an archway here instead of a door," or "If we open up this room, we could install a new patio door out onto a deck." And out come the tools and the measuring tapes, and before you know it, there is an amazing amount of mess and a big hole in the wall.

Our friends all wonder how we can possibly put up with the upheaval, but they are also the first to say, "Gee, I wish we could put in a deck like that." They also quickly learn to avoid visiting during construction if they do not want to learn first-hand how to build a deck.

My father taught woodworking at the local high school, and he has guided us through our projects from the first bookend we ever built to our first attempt at major construction. He also taught geography, and we can recognize most geological landmarks across North America. Words like the Niagara Escarpment and the Laurentian Shield trip easily from our tongues, but that is not quite as usable a skill. Reciprocating saw, cordless drill, laser level—none of those words contain any mystery. We have all poured concrete, raised walls, and gutted rooms. Family discussions and arguments often center on the best construction technique or the endless possibilities of a new floor plan. If you are going to spend any time around my family, eventually we will get you involved in a discussion about some kind of construction, show you the pictures of the project someone just finished or a project one of us is working on or plans for the next one, or we will simply put you to work. Most men would find it surprising to come home and find a backhoe in the front yard, but my husband just sighed and asked if, this time, we could at least keep the indoor plumbing available.

As my sister tried to explain the complicated process of running hidden water lines that had resulted in a heated toilet, my eyes wandered around my new kitchen addition. Dad had built my custom kitchen cabinets from solid pine, and over the years he had helped with ceilings and roofing and windows.

"Did you ever stop to think about how much we owe Dad?" I interrupted Tanya's story. "We would never have been able to do any of this if he had not taught us how to run wiring and install plumbing and build walls. We should thank him for that."

There was a moment of silence on the other end of the phone.

"Without Dad's help, we would have to call in a contractor every time we wanted work done," Tanya said slowly.

Then, I could hear the smile in my sister's voice as she continued with mock indignation. "Do you mean to tell me that we could have had someone come in and tear out the walls and run the plumbing and plaster the drywall and paint and even clean up, and all we would have had to do is write a check? And I could be sitting in the living room with Mom having a glass of wine. This is all Dad's fault? And you want me to thank him? Hah! I should go and swat him."

We both laughed. But we do appreciate the gift that we have been given. Our father gave us the ability to do it ourselves, to create our own world, one that fulfills our dreams and gives us a great sense of accomplishment.

Some gifts never stop.

My brother Mike has his own construction company. He builds new homes and renovates older ones. Dad goes to visit every once in a while and offers advice or a helping hand. The house that my sister Debbie and her husband built themselves on the peak of a mountain towers three stories high and the view from the windows is unbelievable. Dad was there almost every day, sawing lumber and fitting trim.

Tanya's heated toilet is gone now, and her house is returning to its graceful nineteenth-century elegance. She and her husband are also about to start construction on a new building for their business, and Dad has been drawing up floor plans.

My father will turn eighty this year, and as I look around my sprawling home with the built-in library shelves, hand-carved fireplaces, and airy sunroom with the fish pond reflecting the sun streaming through the skylight, I see his hands guiding mine as I made that first crooked bookend.

Now, I need to get back to the tile I'm installing in the kitchen. The tiles will not set properly, and I think I'll call Dad to see if he has any suggestions. I'm sure he will. Then I can do it myself.

—*Gayle Hauver Baillargeon*

# Being Passed by the Little Fellow Who Follows Me

Eighteen years ago, upon the birth of my son, legendary basketball coach John Wooden sent me a copy of a poem he had been presented in 1936 when his own son was born.

Titled, "A Little Fellow Follows Me," it begins:

> *A careful man I want to be,*
> *A little fellow follows me;*
> *I dare not to go astray,*
> *For fear he'll go the self-same way.*\*

I reread the poem often and think of my own little fellow every day—even as he has grown to be more than six feet tall. The poem came to mind again recently when my not-so-little-fellow and I went on a run together.

Like most fathers and sons, we play basketball in the driveway and catch in the park, but The Little Chap Who Follows Me especially likes to run. No—*loves* to run. In the second grade, he even wrote a poem declaring his love of running, aptly titled: "I Am a Boy Who Loves to Run." I am not sure where this pedestrian passion comes from. Track and cross-country were never my sports, nor my two older brothers' sports, nor my dad's. But they are my son's.

My son is much too fast for me these days. He just graduated from high school, where he was a four-year varsity cross-country and track runner who bettered 4:25 in the mile and ran 16 minutes-and-change in the 5K. Now, we only run together occasionally, when he has an "easy" training day as he prepares to run track and cross-country as a freshman at the University of Southern California. Indeed, even though I am fast enough to have qualified for the Boston Marathon, his "easy" runs are my speed workouts just trying to keep up with him!

> *I cannot once escape his eyes,*
> *Whatever he sees me do, he tries;*
> *Like me he says he's going to be,*
> *The little chap who follows me.*

We used to run together a lot. In fact, The Little Chap Who Follows Me actually would run *next* to me. And we talked. A lot. Actually, he talked. Mostly, I listened. He would tell me about his friends, about school, about video games, about what moves he would make if he coached the Lakers.

Our running conversations also included a lot of questions, usually his. Often, his questions made me laugh out loud. Like, "Was Gramps really a kid once?" And "Is Mom growing shorter?"

"What?"

"Dad, I really think she's shrinking!"

"No, I think you're just growing taller."

"Oh, yeah. I guess so."

You can see why I've always savored running with The Little Fellow Who Follows Me, even back when the pace was slower than I would have liked so that he could actually follow me. Admittedly, I knew this wouldn't last long. So it is that, like his shrinking mother, his dad is growing slower.

More than that, the little fellow simply became a faster fellow. Indeed, by age eleven, he could run a 5:37 mile, broke 20 minutes in the 5K, and competed in the cross-country nationals in his age group.

> *He thinks that I am good and fine,*
> *Believes in every word of mine;*
> *The base in me he must not see,*
> *The little chap who follows me.*

I specifically, and fondly, remember one magical day eight years ago—I know the year because it's in my running diary, the memory preserved like a pressed rose in a scrapbook. The Little Chap Who Follows Me wanted to go on a three-mile run. When we reached the turnaround point, I was struggling not to be The Old Man Who Follows Him.

Slowly, but methodically, The Little Fellow Who Follows Me took the lead and widened it.

When he finally sensed that I was no longer with him, he turned around and came back for me. I told him to go ahead and I'd meet him at the park, but he would have none of that and ran alongside me at my pace the rest of the way.

I had envisioned this watershed day coming when I couldn't keep up—but not for another few years, I'd thought. I thought wrong. Indeed, it was no fluke.

A couple days later, we went for a run in the hills and again I struggled to keep pace. Midway up "The Long Monster Hill That Makes Your Legs Burn," as he has nicknamed this stretch of heartbreak road, I breathlessly insisted that he go on ahead and wait for me at the top.

With the summer-like sun setting behind the mountains, I finally crested the Monster Hill—long after The Little Chap Who Follows Me did.

When, at last, I came into his view, he waved at me and smiled a big smile that seemed equal parts I-missed-you-Dad and pride. My pride was even greater.

It is a mental snapshot I will remember as I go through the rest of my summer suns and winter moons.

> *I must remember as I go,*
> *Through summer's sun and winter's snow;*
> *I am building for the years to be*
> *That little chap who follows me.*

Running, of course, is just a metaphor. My then ten-year-old son's flying Nikes as he effortlessly sailed up The Long Monster Hill That Makes Your Legs Burn and left me behind were a reminder of time's winged flight, that The Little Fellow Who Follows Me wouldn't be little for long.

Figuratively, I had glimpsed the future and it is as it should be. Sons should grow taller (at 6 feet, 4 inches, I still have him by two inches! But I grew four inches in college and suspect he may also). And sons should grow faster, stronger, and more talented than their dads. Handsomer, and funnier, and wiser, too. In short, become better. Become, too, careful men with their own little fellows who follow them. Until then, The Little Fellow Who Follows Me gets to lead me. And I couldn't be happier.

—*Woody Woodburn*
**Author unknown*

# Old Red

"Just look at her! Isn't she a beauty?"

I stopped dead in my tracks. Daddy stood next to a totally rusted bike in the basement. It was almost as tall as my five-year-old frame. The seat's padding was gone, and the tires were flat. Who knew what had happened to the kick stand.

"Uh . . . I . . . uh . . ."

"We'll work it over," Daddy added quickly. "It'll be as good as new. We can sand the rust off the frame and handlebars and get some new tires and a seat."

I didn't say anything. This definitely wasn't what I had in mind when I'd asked Daddy for a bicycle.

"What color do you want to paint it? How about red? Real bright red."

"Red? Uh . . . sure. Red's fine," I managed to choke out.

"Found this beauty at the junk yard for two bucks. They said it used to belong to the guy who delivers the *Ft. Scott Tribune*."

My stomach knotted. How could we make this thing look like anything but a piece of junkyard junk? I'd rather walk to school than ride this rusted relic.

"The tires are true. No bends," my dad went on. "I'll pick up some inner tubes at Montgomery Ward on my lunch hour tomorrow and a can of red paint and sandpaper at the paint store. Yes, sir, you'll have a bike by the time first grade starts. Then I can teach you to ride it."

How in the world would I learn to ride such a huge bike? Oh, how I wished I'd kept quiet about wanting a bike.

Daddy continued, "We can work on this together."

Any enthusiasm I might have had drained out my feet.

The next evening while Mom flipped the sizzling pork chops in the frying pan, she looked at me slouched at the kitchen table. "Something wrong, honey?"

I sighed, sat up, and picked at a speck on the tablecloth. "It's just . . . well, I uh, I don't see how Daddy will ever make that bike look like anything, let alone be good enough to ride."

"Honey, there just aren't many bikes to be had right now. Ever since the war, things are in short supply."

The war. Everything seemed to have something to do with the war. Mom and I had to move around the country several times while Daddy served our country in Germany during World War II. He had already completed his voluntary stint in the army ten years before the war ever started. The United States needed men so badly they had drafted Daddy at age thirty-three when I was a year and a half. He didn't come back until after my third birthday. Now, even at five, I still felt a little distanced from him.

Mom came over to the table and put her arm around me. "You know, honey, Daddy might surprise you. He's pretty good at fixing up stuff. You might learn a thing or two from that smart fella."

I wasn't so sure.

Over the next week, my dad and I worked every night after dinner under the light that hung from a rafter in the basement. I sanded the handlebars while Daddy sanded the frame.

"I think we'll be ready to paint by tomorrow night," Daddy said as he brushed off the loose rust with a wire brush.

I thought of the bikes I had seen in the Montgomery Ward catalogue. They sure didn't look anything like this.

"Want to help me paint it? I think I can find another paint brush." Daddy took a screwdriver and pried off the lid of the can labeled "Fire Engine Red."

I shook my head.

He stirred the contents with a paint stick. I'd never seen such a bright red. Well, at least my bicycle would be different from everyone else's. This one wouldn't get to be a light sky blue with white trim like the ones in the catalog. He painted the frame first, then the handlebars. When he finished, he propped it up against the furnace. It didn't look as bad as it had before, but it still needed a seat and a kick stand.

"We'll let this paint dry for a couple of days. While we wait, we can fit the inner tubes into the tires."

I stood back and looked at our project. The handlebars needed handgrips.

The next Saturday, Daddy and I shopped for handlebars, white ones, and chose a brown leather seat. When we got home, he adjusted the seat to the lowest setting and cranked the bolt tight.

"What about a kick stand?" I asked quietly.

"I wasn't able to find one. Don't really need it, anyway. Just lay it down gentle or prop it against a tree." Daddy seemed to have an answer for everything.

He put the wheels on and then the chain.

"Okay, Sally gal, we're ready. Let's give 'er a whirl."

We took the bike out of the basement and into the street. Daddy rode it up and down in front of the house and declared it "Excellent!"

He didn't look too bad on it. Maybe this wasn't such an ugly bike, after all.

I had a little more trouble managing the behemoth, but with Daddy's patient tutoring, I mastered the fine art of bicycle balance. Within the week, I took off down the red brick street without assistance, practicing for my nine-block ride to first grade. The next week, I confidently set off on my first set of wheels for day one at Central grade school in style.

As it turned out, I didn't actually need a seat on the bike for the first year or two; I couldn't sit on the seat and reach the petals at the same time until after third grade. "Old Red," as we affectionately called her, became my first and only bike. I rode it until my teen years. She met her final demise in a fire in the garage. The bike served me well, not only as a means of transportation but also as a way for Daddy and me to reconnect in a deeper way after our wartime separation.

—*Sally Jadlow*

# New Dad + Screaming Baby =
# One Inglorious Spectacle

I can barely hear the woman's question with all the screaming.

"What?" I ask.

I am standing, bouncing really, in a recently refurbished office building. The wood floors are newly varnished. The light is dim. Pretty oil paintings of tranquil scenes with meadows and rivers hang on the wall. And an un-ignorable scream echoes throughout the building.

The woman has come down from upstairs with a look of concern on her face. She motions toward the red-faced baby squirming mightily in my arms. "Is everything all right?"

"Oh. Yes," I assure her.

She doesn't look very assured.

"Just spending some quality time with my son," I offer.

She nods, unconvinced.

I'm not too convinced either.

The idea seemed simple enough: accompany my wife and newborn son into town so she could see her acupuncturist while he and I bonded. The session would take about an hour.

Our bonding experience is now only five minutes old. I am already getting unsolicited concerns from strangers, who, no doubt, could handle the situation better than I.

I am new to fatherhood.

My seemingly simple task has been further complicated by the introduction of the bottle, which happened yesterday. My wife's milk was slow to come in, and so, two weeks after our son's birth, with our newborn starting to lose weight, our midwife encouraged us to supplement his feeding with the bottle and my wife to see her acupuncturist to help with her milk's flow.

The bottles are nice and compact. Slide the clear, plastic inserts in from the top, add warmish, formerly boiled and thus disinfected water, and then scoop in a couple of spoonfuls of powdered formula. Place the nipple securely into the red or blue or green plastic ring, and screw the ring with plastic nipple attachment securely onto the top of the clear, plastic bottle, now complete with sterilized water and correct amount of formula. Finally, snap on the red, blue, or green-colored plastic cap, and shake the entire contraption so that the formula gets mixed in with the water. Be careful to avoid the powder bunching together, especially in the nipple, which can impair the baby's ability to suck the milky formula from the bottle.

The powder isn't bunching together. The baby is still screaming. I take the bottle and angle it downward toward the (quickening) pulse on the underside of my wrist, as I have seen so many mothers and nannies do on TV. The formula does not seem too hot.

The baby screams louder, his bottom lip quivering as tears form in the corners of his overwhelmed eyes.

I elect to take him outside.

Bottle in one hand, screaming baby in the other, Red Sox cap pulled down over my face, I lean in and vigorously make shushing sounds in his ear, as I had read about in *The Happiest Baby on the Block*. This did not have the effect I was hoping for.

Bouncing and shushing under the summer sun in the heat of the parking lot, I spot a shady courtyard with a water fountain. Thinking that the water may be relaxing, we head toward the parking lot oasis.

I take big, bouncing strides, trying to match my energy with my infant son's, another trick I had read about. This only seems to upset him more.

I wonder for a moment what we, specifically I, must look like. I imagine someone instilled with the greatest sense of worry. "Hello, 911? I want to report a suspicious-looking man hiding under a baseball cap, vigorously walking away from a parking lot with a screaming baby in his arms. He doesn't seem very comfortable with the baby. Or vice versa."

We're in downtown Northampton, a college town in Western Massachusetts. The town's motto is, "Where the coffee is strong and so are the women." The phrase is ringing truer and truer by the minute.

Having arrived at our watery oasis, I take a deep, not very reassuring breath, and try to employ my most confident, strong, comforting voice. "Look Myles. Look at the pretty water. Isn't it nice?"

My attempts are greeted with the continued chorus of amplified screams. I bounce more, pacing back and forth. I pull my baseball cap down again, suddenly aware of all the apartment and office windows looking out onto the serene courtyard with the water fountain where a baby is screaming with epic proportion. I am not ready to be a fatherly spectacle.

I have no idea what I'm doing. I put down the bottle. I pick up the bottle. I switch the baby from arm to arm, angle to angle. I bounce, sway, pace, jump, cuddle, and coo. Toward the water fountain, away from the water fountain. The seconds tick by like hours. Try to give him the bottle. Try to give him my finger. Maybe he's not hungry? Maybe he's starving? I have no idea.

Growing tired of the courtyard, we head, again vigorously, back across the parking lot, back into the shelter of the office building, where I am confronted again by the awful echoes of a screaming baby.

I look for a soundproof barrier. It is late, the office doors locked. We opt for the men's room. But it's not very insulating. We return to the hallway.

I'm sweating and exhausted. I can only imagine how Myles feels. I look at my watch. We've been bonding for barely fifteen minutes.

A door opens and the understanding face of the acupuncturist invites us inside. We accept, gratefully, Myles instantly feeling more relaxed. We enter into the treatment room, having crossed into another dimension. Bathed in relaxing greens, soothing music humming in the background, his mother lying comfortably on the patient table with needles sticking out of her calves, he is immediately set to ease. I am, too.

The acupuncturist encourages us to sit down, and my wife shows me how to properly feed our son his bottle. He snuggles comfortably in my arms, calmly staring up at me.

And all is forgiven. We are content.

—*Pete Redington*

# That's My Daddy!

Huge tears rolled down tiny cheeks as I sat in the cool grass of the neighbor's lawn, hugging my swelling foot. I was only five years old the day I stepped on that hornet. A handsome man dashed to my rescue from across the street. He scooped me up into strong, loving arms and carried me home. He covered the sting with baking soda paste. Then he made me his cure for everything: a bowl of chocolate ice cream stirred until it was creamy. "Soft-serve" style, he called it.

That memory and a few tattered photographs were all I had of my father growing up. My parents divorced, and he disappeared, leaving an empty space where a father should be. I did not think I would ever know or be able to find him. That is, until I discovered the Internet.

On my thirtieth birthday I received a used computer, and I soon discovered people-search programs on the World Wide Web. I typed in my father's name and sat in silent anticipation as the computer blinked and whirred.

I was shocked to see that the name was in the database. A list of twenty or so, complete with telephone numbers, appeared on the screen. I hesitated for what seemed like hours. Finally, I reached for the telephone.

The first telephone number on the list was disconnected. I dialed the second number. There was no answer. Finally, when I dialed the third telephone number, a deep voice answered the telephone. He lived in Colorado Springs, Colorado, a long way from my home in southern Oregon.

"Hello, I'm looking for someone with the same name as yours," the words rushed out of my mouth before I could lose my nerve. "May I ask you a question?"

"Sure," came the cheerful reply.

I took a deep breath and continued. "May I ask where you grew up?"

His answer stunned me. He named the town in Oregon where my family originated and where I still lived.

"Who is this?" The deep voice asked a little nervously.

"This is Tisha." My voice sounded strange all of a sudden.

"Tisha Railene?" he gasped.

"Yes."

The line went silent for a moment. Then I heard a sob catch in his throat as he answered. "You know, when you were a little girl I used to call you 'Angel.'"

I knew that. Mom didn't mention him much as we were growing up, but that was one thing she'd told me.

"I've been celebrating your birthday every year," he added, his voice still wavering with emotion. "Your sister's, too."

Now, I was crying too.

Through our tears, we talked for hours, catching up on more than thirty lost years. By the end of our conversation, we were making plans for him to fly out and visit.

Early the following morning, I phoned Clare, who lived a few miles from me.

"I found our father, and I don't mean the one who art in heaven. And he's coming to visit us."

"Great," she said flatly.

Clare was less than thrilled, understandably. My sister is always slow to warm to new ideas. And our father hadn't been much of a father to us. Indeed, three decades had gone by since we'd seen him. But he was a missing piece in the puzzle of my life, and I was anxious to learn about my heritage and my early childhood.

Christmas morning that year found my sister Clare and I standing in the airport terminal with some news journalists who had heard about the reunion. Clare picked her split ends and I chewed off my fingernails as we waited for the board to announce the arrival of his flight.

"How will we know it's him?" Clare asked as the passengers began to file off the plane.

I was thinking of a response when, suddenly, all doubt was lost. We spotted him, the last passenger to leave the plane, and there was no mistake. A tall Native American man with a long gray braid paused to tease one of the flight attendants before turning to us. A sign hung around his neck; in sparkling blue letters about four inches tall was one word: "DAD."

Amidst cameras flashing and a crowd of applauding onlookers, our father stepped forward and tucked one of us under each arm as tears flowed again. I looked up shyly as he leaned down to kiss me on the forehead. So this was Daddy.

"So you haven't seen your girls or Southern Oregon in over thirty years," one reporter asked Dad. "What will you do first?"

Dad hesitated only a moment. "We've got a lot of catching up to do," he paused to hug us both again. "I think I'll take my girls out for some chocolate ice cream, soft-serve style."

Before Dad returned to Colorado, we went out for an evening of karaoke. By then, Clare was still a little withdrawn but was beginning to warm up to him. My heart filled with pride as he stood on the stage and told everyone of our reunion. Then, I went up to join him on stage, and with Clare cheering us on, we sang "Somewhere Out There." To this day, that is "our song."

A few months after our reunion, Clare and I took a train to Colorado, where we helped Dad pack up everything he owned in two trucks and a car. We headed West in a caravan with a sign on the back of Dad's trailer that read "Oregon or Bust."

Now, we live in the same town and spend as much time together as possible. Sometimes, friends who see us approach and ask me who my new friend is. I proudly answer, "That big ol' bear? That's my daddy!"

—*Tea Coiner Harris*

# How to Stop the Rain
# and Other Small Miracles

Many years ago, when I was a little girl of about ten, I discovered that my father can stop the rain. I was nestled in my cozy daybed underneath my favorite flowered comforter, and the rain was hammering so loudly outside my bedroom window that I grew scared and couldn't sleep. I was a child who watched the news, and lying in my bed that night, images of storm-ravaged towns and flooded streets filled my head, and I was convinced that at any moment the roof would cave in and I would be swept away.

After what seemed like ages, I finally called out softly to my dad—please, please could he come fix it, make it go away?

Just calling for him made me feel better. After all, I knew my dad, and he could fix anything.

My dad is a mechanical engineer by training and a brilliant inventor by nature. His brain and hands can make anything happen. He's designed irrigation projects to water the deserts, built lasers that fix eyes and other lasers that fix anything from a racer bike to an airplane. He can make robots move, electricity flow, and wood planks come together to form box cars for his kids. So, it was perfectly understandable that, in my ten-year-old brain, my dad could fix anything on Earth—including stopping the driving rain that was terrifying me.

It was late at night and I was supposed to be sleeping. In the next room, my parents were watching *60 Minutes*. I could hear the *tick, tick, tick* of its introduction and the TV voices droning on and on, very much the way the rain sounded outside—constant, jarring.

Normally, I enjoyed the sound of the rain. I liked the gurgling sound it made when it hit puddles and the cheerful sound it made, like fairies clapping, when it fell softly on trees and rooftops. Many times while walking home from school, I'd been caught in a rain shower and would stop and stand under my umbrella watching the rain fall all around me, bouncing off my umbrella, creating a small waterfall around me. Usually, I found the rain to be comforting and almost magical.

But in my bed that night, with the rain hammering down all around me, the thunder clapping loudly and the lightning flashing outside my window like a burglar's flashlight, I did not like the rain at all. This was no lovely little rain shower; it was a scary, monstrous rainstorm. The rain fell so heavily that it sounded like a thousand big, strong men were standing out in our yard pounding on giant steel drums.

Eight years later, I would learn to sleep through dorm noises far more alarming than steel-drum rain, but at ten and living in a quiet suburb, I was a light sleeper and accustomed to quiet nights.

I called out again to my dad, louder this time. And this time, he heard me. Within a minute, he appeared at my doorway, silhouetted like a superhero in the door frame.

My dad is an imposing figure. Not quite six feet tall, he's not actually a giant, but he has the stature and stance of someone who thinks tall. I think I inherited this quality from him—of course, thinking tall at my height (all of five feet nothing) is a little more ridiculous. Nevertheless, I have always felt tall, and I owe that to my dad, who taught me to hold myself with dignity and calm confidence. He never said as much to me, but I'd learned to "stand tall" from his example—from seeing how his pride and intelligence had carried him through those hard times when he was struggling to make his business a success from the basement of our house.

Back then, Dad would wake up early every morning, take his usual jog, and do what he called "gymnastics" but was actually yoga, before yoga became cool. Then he would shower and get dressed in slacks, shirt, and tie, eat a quick breakfast, and walk his short commute down the stairs to his basement office. To be honest, the tie always puzzled me, being as the accessory had no apparent use other than to make an outfit appear professional and, in those early months of the business, on most days my father saw no one but our cat all day.

Over the years, my father's genius and hard work pushed the business out of our basement and into an old mill in Lowell, a ninety-minute drive from our house. My dad rose early, drove the distance, worked hard, and made it home for dinner every night. This was always extremely important to him, and when he came home, we all felt that he was back with us. After kissing and hugging us all hello, he would immediately take off his tie and change into his home clothes. When we saw him come into the kitchen wearing sweatpants and a sweatshirt, we knew he had left work behind and was all ours.

Though my father's career was important to him and he worked too hard and many hours, I never felt neglected or abandoned. I never felt that his work came first, that it was an amorphous alien that sucked up all of my father's time and attention. Dad somehow always made it clear that the work was for us, for our family, as well as for him. And he always made it a point to be a part of our daily lives, to be there with and for us. One day, he quietly mentioned in passing that he had named the business after us, using our initials in the company title. All those little things that he did and said told us that we were always in his thoughts, that we were, in fact, the center of his world.

Now that I'm grown, married, and living farther away from my parents than I would like, I still think about those days when I lived in our old house and slept in my flower-covered daybed. I remember my dad making it home from work for dinner and coming to the table in his home clothes and a smile, and I find myself rushing for the closet when I come home, too, peeling off the layers of work and changing into home clothes to really be there, to be present, with my husband for the evening or the weekend. My husband and I hope to start a family of our own someday, and we're both determined to model our lives after my dad's example—to work hard, but to be there for each other and our future children.

We also make a habit of calling our parents every week. Although we may not get to talk as often or as long as we'd like, we make a point to talk, to share the little idiosyncrasies of our days with them and to take an interest in their days too.

My husband and I work long hours, but, following my father's lifelong example, we do not let it consume us and we make time for one another and for our family. My dad and his company are facing hard times again, just as much of the country is. So, instead of retiring, Dad is still running his business, still fixing things, still helping his employees put food on their families' tables, and still sending them home in time to eat that food with their kids and spouses. Now, he's not just my superhero, he's theirs too.

My father can stop the rain.

When I was ten, I called for my dad to stop a terrible rainstorm. He went outside in the pouring rain, covered the metal gutter outside my window with rags to muffle the noise, and came back inside to kiss me goodnight. Sometimes, it's the little things that matter most.

*—Hanna R. Neier*

# A Dad for All Seasons

"Dad, here, now!" Allie demands imperiously, gesturing broadly with her arms.

Glancing back over her shoulder impatiently, she hurries purposefully toward the kitchen.

"Pie ready now! Open oven," she enthusiastically instructs her beloved daddy.

As her father opens the oven door and removes the golden brown pumpkin pie, Allie claps her hands excitedly and cheers her approval.

"Wow, wow—hot pie!"

Born ten years ago with Down syndrome, Allie has faced a number of significant challenges in her life. After three open-heart operations, a stroke, and numerous medical emergencies, she is now relatively strong and healthy. Her father retired from his job as a mechanical engineer a year ago, and the months since then have been a time of exploration and bonding for father and daughter.

On this beautiful fall morning at our home in the Sierra Nevada foothills, Dad and Allie baked their first pie. Carefully following a favorite family recipe, they scooped pumpkin pie filling from the can, cracked open several large eggs, added evaporated milk, and stirred in pungent spices. Allie vigorously mixed the pie filling while Dad rolled out the crust on the floured cutting board. Amidst clouds of flour and flying scraps of dough, Allie and Dad fashioned the crust into a rough circle and gingerly transferred it to a pie tin. Then Allie splashed the creamy filling into the crust with gusto and grinned broadly at her Dad.

"Pie ready now. Go, Dad!"

He obediently lifted the pie into the oven while Allie set the kitchen timer for thirty minutes.

"There," Allie announced proudly as she shook flour from her striped apron, "Good job, Dad. Good job, Allie."

It was, indeed, a good job. While my husband Ron has always been involved in raising Allie and our two older children, this frail daughter with her marked differences has been a bit overwhelming for him. Much of her infancy was spent in the intensive care unit of the university medical center. Born with an immature immune system, Allie developed infection after infection. Finally, though, her health stabilized, and now she is ready and able to go about the business of everyday living.

Ron retired early in part to spend more time with Allie and to help with her education. We had decided years ago to home school Allie through a local charter school program, and our home is a learning laboratory. As Allie's primary teacher, I've been teaching her reading, social studies, math, science, and art all of her life. She receives weekly visits from a variety of specialists—occupational therapists, speech and language pathologists, adaptive physical education teachers, physical therapists, and special education resource teachers. Each professional urges us to carry out stimulating activities between weekly visits, so there's always plenty to do with Allie.

When he first retired, Ron enthusiastically tackled the long list of learning experiences we had written out for Allie. Excited and ready to make a difference in Allie's life, he was stunned to discover that his youngest daughter didn't seem to share his enthusiasm and commitment.

"No way!" Allie politely but firmly responded whenever her dad suggested an educational activity. "Mom do."

Her message was quite clear: Daddy was fine for fun and games, but learning and schoolwork belonged to Mom. Whenever Ron persisted, Allie would cry miserably and turn toward me in despair. "Mom turn. Dad go play."

Ron read some books on parenting and dutifully pumped me for ideas that would spark Allie's interest and hold her attention. As he continued working with Allie, he developed his own style and the two of them found new interests in common. Slowly but surely, the father-daughter duo reached a tentative truce and then formed a permanent alliance.

Surprisingly enough, the first breakthrough came in the form of a science kit we had purchased so Allie could learn about machines. With gears, string, and rubber bands, Dad and Allie built a miniature tram that slowly and majestically traveled across our living room and down the stairs on a wire.

When asked who had built the wonderful tram, Allie proudly announced, "Allie do. Dad, too!"

From that point on, they were like two mad scientists in their quest to learn more about the world.

The tram was quickly followed by a ringing doorbell, a telegraph, and a hand-held electric fan. Elated with their successes, Dad and Allie decided to raise miniature frogs and monarch butterflies. They purchased kits at the local teachers' supply store and dutifully mailed in the postcards that would bring cocoons and tadpoles in the mail. Each day, they walked down our driveway hand in hand to the mailbox. One memorable day, they hurried back up the steps. Clutching the tiny box against her chest, Allie burst into the house, "Mom, Mom, frog here." Together, Dad and Allie assembled the habitat and released the wriggling tadpole into the water. Day after day, they monitored its growth and development until it grew into a small brown frog.

Once the science projects created a bond, Dad and Allie moved on to other areas of learning and exploration. Allie's speech was significantly impaired as a result of the Down syndrome and the stroke she had at age three. Cheerful and outgoing, she communicated with a combination of sign language, facial expressions, and gestures supplemented with a few precious words. Dad and Allie sat together for hours playing speech games and practicing the sounds that were so very difficult for her mouth to pronounce. Looking intently into the mirror, Allie hugged Dad and laboriously forced her tongue to the top of her mouth. "La," she enunciated carefully, "La, la." Together, Dad and Allie worked to make the sounds that Allie could then form into words. Slowly but surely, her speech improved until she could say several words in a row.

Year round, Dad and Allie learned and grew together. The warm California summer was a favorite time. Towel and goggles in hand, bodies coated with sunscreen, they headed to the community pool, where Allie dove and glided happily through the cool turquoise water. Together, they spent a week at a Girl Scout camp in the Sierra Nevada Mountains, learning Native American games and crafts. When the wind picked up, they grabbed their life jackets and sailed back and forth across a small manmade lake.

When the leaves began to turn red and gold, Dad and Allie drove up to Apple Hill and came back with armloads of crisp red apples and bright orange pumpkins. Soon the kitchen was filled with the cinnamon scent of their baked apples. They cut open the pumpkins and scooped out handfuls of slippery seeds. Laughing uproariously, they carved fiendish faces in each and inserted small candles before arranging them artfully on our front porch.

Winter brought outdoor fun in the snow at Lake Tahoe. Bundling up against the cold, Dad and Allie headed up for a day of snowmen, snowballs, and sledding. Filling a cooler with snow, they headed home to share the winter festivities with the rest of the family. A cup of hot cocoa and a warm bath revived a tired Allie and got her ready for an evening of Monopoly or Sorry.

Spring brought brisk winds, which called for kites! Together, Dad and Allie built a large colorful kite that looked like a ship in full sail. Off to the local park they went, to fly it high in the cloudy sky. When raindrops fell, they hurried home to make cookies and cakes out of colorful clay for a fantasy tea party.

And always, there was more learning to be done! With her new tape measure in hand, Allie measured doorways, boxes, and even the family cats. Allie and Dad built a weather station and solemnly recorded data about temperature and rainfall. They dissected starfish, worms, and grasshoppers and made precise drawings in Allie's biography notebook. Side by side on the sofa, they pored over picture books about pioneers, ships, animals, explorers, and the environment.

Allie's life today is fuller and richer because of the time she's spent working and learning with her father. No longer just a playmate, Dad is now a beloved teacher, fellow scientist, and engineering buddy. Winter, summer, spring, or fall, he truly is a dad for all seasons.

*—Sandy Keefe*

# Attack of the Killer Ducks

It's Tuesday! Playgroup time!

I love taking my fifteen-month-old daughter to the Tuesday playgroup at our local church. It's a chance for Clara to socialize with her chubby peers and for my wife to take a couple of hours off.

This is the only playgroup in our area where I feel welcome. All the other playgroups in town are actually called "moms' groups," which presents me with a gender barrier. I once approached a mom about crashing one of these groups; she didn't say no, but she didn't sound overly enthusiastic about the idea, either. In the end, I wasn't brave enough to try it.

While I haven't seen many dads at the church playgroup, at least they aren't barred by the playgroup's title. So I take Clara every chance I get.

Going to playgroup is never a sure thing because it's tricky getting my daughter to leave the house with only me. If I play my cards wrong in trying to extract Clara from her mother, they will both end up sobbing, so I've learned not to force the issue.

But today Clara is good to go. All I have to do is make a few car noises, and she waddles over to the front door and loudly air-kisses her mother goodbye with a smack of her tiny hand, like a movie star leaving a party.

By the time we get to the car, Clara is practically vibrating. This is, in part, because she knows I'll play Johnny Mathis's version of "Sleigh Ride," her favorite, on continuous repeat all the way over. Luckily, it's a short ride.

As we park at the church lot, I remind myself to be polite and to try talking to the other adults in the group. This is the one downside to Tuesday playgroup. I love playing with Clara and the other toddlers, but I usually find conversations with their parents to be a great cure for insomnia.

Playgroup parents have little in common with each other besides the fact that we've all produced offspring. Since it's not polite to talk about how we accomplished this, there's nothing left to discuss but the offspring themselves. This means all conversation essentially boils down to an endless comparison of notes:

> **Parent 1:** "Lisa started crawling at nine months."
> **Parent 2:** "Really? Jesse started around ten."
> **Parent 1:** "No kidding."
> **Parent 2:** "Yup."

A conversation like this might drag on indefinitely and can only be broken up by a child falling down and crying. Most playgroup veterans seem happy to talk like this, but I can't carry the conversation for more than a few seconds. Either I blissfully stare at my daughter and forget I'm interacting with someone or I try in vain to focus on the conversation until drool trickles out of my mouth.

But when we step into the church hall, we find a joyous surprise: there aren't any other parents inside, only the playgroup leader. This might have led to even more strained conversation, except the playgroup leader happens to be Clara's grandmother. I couldn't be happier. Neither can Clara. She soon grasps the idea that she has both Grammy and a room full of new toys all to herself, and she quickly gets to work.

What follows is the most focused and complex game my daughter has ever initiated. First, she takes out all the animals from the toy box and hands them to Grammy, giving each animal an appropriate sound. The sounds may not be species-specific (all the snarling tigers sound like housecats, except for a few that sound like dogs), but they're pretty good for a fifteen-month-old. Once the toy animals are all lined up, Clara gives each of them something to eat or drink on little plastic plates and cups. The menu, restricted to items in her food vocabulary, consists of chocolate, apples, milk, tea, and tofu. Tea turns out to be a particular favorite among the plastic tigers, while one of the rubber ducks prefers munching on the face of a small plastic boy. The implications of such a sight are staggering.

Grammy and I watch in bemused, if slightly horrified, silence, only occasionally stirring to hand over the next plate of tofu for the elephants.

Such a game could never exist in a room full of toddlers; the tigers would have been scattered to the four winds in seconds. Nor could I have shielded Clara from such intrusions; I would have been too distracted by well-meaning parents asking me when Clara first let us put a hat on her. (The answer: never.)

Maybe, at least for this week, socialization with one's peers is overrated. But I'll never look at ducks the same way again.

—*Craig Idlebrook*

# Entranced

It is peculiar to who I am to stare at things a lot. In the sixties this behavior was referred to as "contemplating one's navel," which I could never do because I had no interest in the subject. But if you, my darling, were a belly button, what a happy hippie I could be.

I inherited this propensity toward focused vision from your grandmother, who sadly passed away when I was just seventeen. She was particularly keen on staring at me after preparing my breakfast. She would sit at the kitchen table watching me devour mouthfuls of her scrumptious apple-cinnamon pancakes.

Finally, I would break concentration on what I was chewing long enough to whine, "Mama, quit staring at me."

After I'd scold her in this manner, she would pretend to busy herself, fidgeting at the corner of the tablecloth or straightening a place setting, but would be at it again a few seconds later.

"Why do you do that, Mama?" I would ask.

"I just like to look at you," was her simple reply.

I didn't begin to comprehend the significance of her explanation until God blessed me with you. I've learned so much this year from you and your mom, who, by the way, is absolutely amazing. She has been your constant companion, teaching you colors and songs, dancing with you, fixing boo-boos, anticipating and responding to your needs with a strength and devotion that has forever clarified the meaning of maternal love for me.

Last night, we all went to the buffet-style restaurant. I remember your mom saying how pleasant it was as we strolled past the smaller shops to the large department store to exchange two play shirts you got last week for your second birthday. It wasn't until we were actually in the store that your mom mentioned she wasn't exactly sure these clothes were from this store, but she thought they probably were. Now, a great meal tends to soften a man's mind and his resolve for a short time, so it was with zombie-like compliance that I picked you up and obediently began shuffling through racks of tops, looking for a match to our return.

Your mother soon recognized the futility of this effort as rows of clothes stretched out endlessly before us. Or maybe she saw that I was becoming semi-conscious and had that "what in the world am I doing here and how can I get out of it fast?" look on my face.

You were way ahead of me. You gave up just the slightest burp followed by two demure little coughs. You rocked your head toward my chest and then away—politely taking aim so as not to offend other customers—and barfed all over me in a heave-ho tidal wave, while I stood hopelessly helpless in the aisle. That got your mom's attention.

She was second in line at the checkout counter and appeared, from my vantage point, to be somewhat reluctant to relinquish her position. However, once she understood our plight, she was by our side and following my instructions: "Take the keys from my pocket and meet us outside with the car." By the time your third and final projection began, we were nearly to the door.

We parked ourselves on the curb as inconspicuously as possible, downwind from strangers—me naked to my shorts and you to your diaper. It probably seems wacko that I preferred being there with you and encrusted in vomit than in the purgatory of the department store.

"That was a pretty clever idea," I said. "But maybe when you're a bit older we can work more closely on the plan."

"Yeah," you responded happily.

Friends who are parents have told me that each new stage of a child's life is often better than the last, but I have never faced change easily. When my wife said it was time to take your crib down earlier this year, I cried while I did it. And not because I'd pinched my finger. And I didn't merely shed one or two manly tears. I found the experience to be devastating, but it also led to what has become my most cherished moments with you.

Sometimes, while in your new bed, you wake up in the night in need of comfort, and on the occasion when I can beat your mom out of our bed, I hurry to your side with a bottle and a shoulder to share. As we lie there, at first I am fooled into thinking I am holding you, but soon I realize you are holding me. In the darkness, you gently run your fingers over my face, exploring its structure. Then you might direct my arm across your body to gently pinch my elbow or squeeze my knuckles, or simply pass your hand back and forth over my forearm. There is no velvet as soft and smooth as your touch as you eventually drift off to sleep.

Then, in the morning, I very much like watching you wake up. Rolling from back to stomach, you stretch and then bury your head into the pillow with your bottom high in the air like a turtle trying to hide in the sand.

I lean in close to your ear and whisper, "Kayla, do you know Daddy loves you?"

You nod your head ever so slightly in affirmation, content enough with the knowledge to enjoy just a few more minutes of peaceful slumber.

Equally thrilling is how, when you're up and about, I'll stop and say "Kayla" to get your attention.

"Do you know who is Daddy's favorite little girl?" I ask.

Even before I can finish the question, you shout, "Me!"

So forgive me if, every once in a while, I stare at you. I am entranced by your presence. Sometimes, I am seeing you through your grandmother's eyes, and I finally understand the pleasure to be found in so doing. But mostly these long peeks are for me.

—*Samuel P. Clark*

*This story was first published in* In My Shoes, *Summer 1996, a small-distribution periodical that ceased publication in 1996.*

# A Hero's Welcome

It never fails. At exactly 5:01 P.M. every work day, my daughters start getting antsy. A few minutes later, the coughing and sputtering of an old worn engine signals that our car is rounding the corner to our townhouse. Just like at the starter's gate at a horse race, the sounds of the squeaky brakes setting and one last rev of the engine cause the girls to stop whatever activity (or fighting) they're doing and wait for the sound of the gun to go off. There it is: the keys in the lock! And they're off!

"Daddy!" they scream in unison.

"Hi there, girls," he laughs.

He barely gets in the door before tiny arms wrap around his legs, clinging to him like little koala bears. They don't even notice the gasoline smell sticking to his clothes that our old jalopy leaves from the ride home.

"Spin me! Spin me!" Jordhan screeches.

"No! Me first!" Jaimie forces herself in front of the line.

Honestly, it warms the cockles of my heart—whatever and wherever those are—to see the girls so happy to see their daddy. He's so tender with them, even when they're "rough-housing." Each night he comes home tired, stressed, fed up about his job. Yet, he always musters up enough energy to burn off with his girls.

"Tag! You it, Daddy!" Jaimie giggles as she runs up the stairs.

"Oh . . . I'm gonna getcha!" he teases.

A high-pitched squeal responds from above us.

He grabs Jordhan, flips her upside down and over his shoulder, and races up the stairs.

On my mommy resume, I am disciplinarian, chef, chauffeur, nurse, referee, bodyguard, maid, entertainer, scary dream calmer, and monster-under-the-bed eliminator. I kiss boo-boos, answer questions (oh so many questions), and can change a diaper in less than two minutes (when the subject lies still). And yet, I get no hero's welcome like daddy does.

Then again, I spend every waking moment with them while he only has a few hours each day and a day on the weekend. Every time, he plays with them as though it's the first and last time he'll ever play with them again. I can see sadness in his chocolate brown eyes as he leaves each morning.

"Daddy's going to work now, sweet peas," he says with a weak smile. "You be good for Mama."

"Buh-bye, Dadee," says Jordhan with a big smile.

Then we wave to him from the kitchen window as the car sputters and coughs him to work.

His girls mean the world to him, and I know his excitement at seeing them at the end of the day is genuine. I think he misses them. That's not all he misses.

I heard Jordhan's first laugh; I got to experience the first time both girls took their first steps; I was the cheering section when Jaimie went on the potty the first time. Their daddy only heard about these milestones later. It's Mama who the girls want to comfort them, to kiss their owies and to kiss them goodnight. And, for some reason, they never remember Daddy's name when they wake up in the middle of the night.

Still, Daddy receives the Hero's Welcome every day.

Their hero is home for the night, and the welcome party continues upstairs. I hear the small stampede passing over my head, followed by the sound of little bodies bouncing on our bed. Suddenly, there's a much louder banging as Daddy joins the trampoline act. Then a crash. Silence.

"Daddy breaked da bed, Mama! Daddy breaked da bed!" Jaimie tattles from the top of the stairs.

Wonderful.

As I go up the stairs to investigate—and to reprimand Daddy for jumping on the bed and breaking it, again—I mask a smile as I hear Daddy whispering (loud enough for me to hear), "*Shhh*, you're gonna get Daddy in trouble."

It doesn't seem to matter if Daddy gets into trouble or what happens now, because tomorrow when he comes home, he'll get the Daddy Hero's Welcome again. This is the special relationship that Daddies and daughters share. And these are the stories he'll share on the day he tearily gives their hands to the other man in their hearts.

Until then, maybe we should just take the mattresses off the bed frame.

—*Chynna Tamara Laird*

# Turtle Tears

I have always admired my big brother, Jason. Even though, growing up, he was the oldest in a family of five children, he always had time for me, his younger sister. When he was three and I was one, he even saved my life. We were playing at the beach, and I went under and was being swept away. My mother ran for me but couldn't see me through the churned-up sand. Jason, strong even then, saw the blue gingham of my bathing suit flash by, and he reached in and pulled me up.

Jason taught me how to ride my bike by holding on and not letting go until he was sure I was ready. He had a sense of humor and timing that would send soda spitting through my girlfriends' noses.

When he was a senior in high school and I was a freshman, he drove me to school every day. He listened to my woes and triumphs, gave me the heads-up on teachers and on which boys to avoid, and he reminded me, as an all-knowing senior, that high school lasted only four years. He played on the football team in the fall and threw shot put in the spring; he worked different jobs on Saturday; and he served as an altar boy on Sunday morning.

When a new family moved into the neighborhood, I giggled as I watched Jason fall in love with the girl next door. He hemmed and hawed around her for the summer and then went off to college. Every visit home, he became a little more confident around Cheryl. He came back to take her to her senior prom, and the rest, as they say, is history. I was a bridesmaid at their wedding and saw up-close how deeply he had won the heart of such a beautiful bride. I was at all four of their children's christenings.

But, if I had to pick one moment when I really saw my brother for the man he is, it was when I saw him for the father he is.

It was on Turtle Races Day in Longville, Minnesota, a town of 180 people. A hot August day made for children—full of popcorn, cotton candy, loud music, games, double scoop ice creams, and hot dogs. A day we had all enjoyed throughout our childhood, when we would come to our grandparent's lakefront home for vacation and "go into town" for the weekly turtle races.

The years had passed, and now Jason and I were the parents, reliving the magic of it all through the eyes of our children. Quarters were handed out, turtles inspected, ice cream flavors picked, bathroom lines waited in, and hands washed. The cousins tossed bean bags, guessed candy numbers in jars, and did the chicken dance while my brother and I waited—and waited and waited and waited—in the sun-intense line to register each of them for the races. I gained a new appreciation for the parental side of Turtle Race Day!

Only Jason's daughter Joy didn't want to race. She begged with glistening tears not to have to touch one of those "turdly things." Jason reassured her that it was fun, that turtles were people-friendly, that he would touch the turtle for her. But have any of these arguments ever been known to change the mind of a three-year-old girl? They didn't work this time, either.

After thirty minutes of inching forward in line, we made it to the front, paid the registration fees, and received our racing numbers, corresponding turtles, and souvenir pins. When we were done, Joy gathered with all the cousins, watched their numbers being pinned on their shirts and the turtles in their holding tanks, then looked up at her daddy with tears filling her big blue eyes again.

"Joy, you don't have to race a turtle, honey," my brother reassured her.

Tears started free flowing. "But I want to," she said gently. "Do you think I still could?" She asked with all the tender trust of a little girl with her father. "I'm not afraid of those turdly things anymore."

Jason looked at the long registration line and then back at his daughter. I saw his conflict between giving her the same summertime memories he'd had and his dread of waiting in the long line again in the summertime heat. The conflict lasted all of a few seconds.

My brother just smiled and took his place at the end of the line.

*—Cynthia Hamond as told by Renee Swanson*

# Awake

The massive double bed swallowed my small, five-year-old frame. At bedtime, I made sure to lie squarely in the middle so that no monsters' arms could reach me from beneath. All was dark except for the tiny bulb of the hallway's fire detector, blazing red like the beady eyes of the creatures that schemed their attack on me. Sleep eventually overtook my fears. Then . . .

*Click.*

The main hall light flashed on. It happened every Monday morning, long before the sun came up. So unusual a nighttime noise and so bright a beam were sure to startle any other kid my age, but I remained calm and still, simply waiting for what happened next. Yes, it could have been any of the various freaks and ghosts and ghouls that haunted my bedroom whenever the sky turned dark. But in the wee hours of the morning, this was the one silhouette that didn't trigger the thought of spooks.

His boots echoed across the bedroom's hardwood floor. As he approached, I smelled a million miles of oil and exhaust caught up in his army-green work coat. I drowsily threw off the covers, sat up as best I could, and stretched out my arms for a hug.

"Goodbye, Barbie. I love you," he said.

"Bye. I love you too, Daddy."

He re-tucked my blankets around me as I nestled back into the center of my bed. He made his way toward the hallway, and with a flip of a switch, all was black again.

For more than thirty years, my father was a truck driver. Dad was on the road Monday through Friday, which made weekends and his annual three weeks of vacation his only opportunities for any kind of home life. He missed most of my musical performances, parent-teacher conferences, and sporting events. He rarely witnessed the spectacle of proud moments, occasional tantrums, and childhood antics of all kinds. For all of my growing up, he entrusted my mother to the daily grind of my discipline, care, and feeding. But I was none the wiser that my life was somehow lacking.

Though countless articles, investigative news reports, and psychological studies claim the importance of a very present and involved father, I'm not one of the statistics who somehow feels slighted because of my dad's frequent physical absence. Instead, this one gesture more than made up for his time away: the routine and tenderness of those Monday mornings.

"Don't wake the baby" is a popular mantra among new parents. They understand and dread the consequences if naptimes are missed or, God forbid, nighttime is mistaken for day. Even though their children don't remain babies for long, parents still seem to profess and apply those age-old words of wisdom. They also quickly learn that there's much to be said for knowing that their three-year-old or twelve-year-old or eighteen-year-old is sleeping safely and soundly at home in bed.

But, no matter my age, Dad woke me in the middle of the night, not to rescue me from monsters or a fire or some other calamity, but for an altogether different reason: to offer a hug and to tell me he loved me. What others might have thought preposterous became precious between father and daughter.

In my case, the consequences of "waking the baby" were bound to become more disastrous as I grew older. Like Forrest Gump and his box of chocolates, Dad never knew what he was going to get whenever he was around me. I eventually joined the ranks of other teenage girls—mouthy, spiteful, and entirely rebellious adolescents whose parents often fall prey to the rage of adolescent hormones. "I hate you," I'd scream as my father denied me the car keys or embarrassed me with his wardrobe, his hair, or anything else that I deemed uncool. Flipping my middle finger, slamming doors, shouting expletives— I threw stones of all kinds during my frequent fits of teen temper.

But then came Monday morning.

My lanky sixteen-year-old frame stretched from edge to edge of the old double bed, my orthodontic headgear making its characteristic dents in the pillows as I slept. My room was decorated in floor-to-ceiling photographs of beachscapes and other far-away places, hunky rock stars in all their teased-hair glory, and my favorite prom dresses clipped from the latest *Seventeen* magazine. In the very early morning, such teenage treasures were absorbed in shadow until . . .

*Click.*

The hall light came on, and a familiar shape filled the doorway of my corner bedroom. Heavy work boots trudged across worn wood. He muttered and cursed in his unsuccessful attempts to dodge tall piles of rejected clothing, crinkled magazines, and high school textbooks. A million more miles of oil and exhaust had penetrated his work jacket. No matter what shenanigans I'd pulled throughout the weekend, Dad bent down to wrap me in the same hug as last Monday, the Monday before, and the Monday before that.

"See you on Friday, Barb. I love you."

"Okay. Love ya too."

Our usual goodbye. And despite my shameful behavior toward Dad throughout the weekend, I knew he still meant it. I did too.

Many years have passed since those early Monday morning goodbyes. Today, several of my friends confide that they've never heard their fathers say "I love you." Never. But with the flip of a switch and a ten-second ritual, my story is amazingly different and blessed. The world said, "Don't wake the baby," but how grateful I am that Dad acted against such "wisdom." As a result, I'm fully awake to the depth of my father's love—and, even though it might defy popular conventions, I hope to pass his sweet legacy on to my own children.

*—Barbara Farland*

# The Old
# Tin Train

According to my stepdad, Joe, his tin train was over eighty-seven years old. Rusted in only a few creases, it rattled down the tracks we puzzled together just before Christmas every year, until my Mom painted a piece of plywood kelly green—his favorite color—and nailed the tracks into a permanent layout. She always chose a blue spruce to stand in the center of the track for the train to lap around. My little brother and I knew we were not to touch any part of the train or the transformer, and we truly tried not to.

We were allowed to watch, though. It was a few years before my brother and I figured out why the train would go one way down the track, but on its next lap, turn magically around and go the other way. Joe played on this mystery, encouraging our predictions.

"It's going left!" I would say.

"No, it's going right!" my brother would counter.

Little did we know that Joe could control a switch in the track to make it go either direction.

"You were right," I would have to admit to my brother.

"I know, and this time it's going left," he'd say.

Joe would flip the switch so it would go left. Or just let it go right until we were convinced that was the direction it should be going in, then he'd flip the switch and make it go left.

After this game had gone on for a while—typically punctuated by my brother and I arguing over which way the train would go next—Mom would call out, "Time for bed."

We'd tear ourselves away from the display to kiss our parents goodnight, race to our beds, and hop in. Always.

Only one time can I remember getting to stay up past bedtime. I still don't know how that happened. Everyone else had gone to bed, but Joe was lying on his stomach watching his old train go around the track. I sat with him, cross-legged on the hardwood floor, my long flannel nightgown pinched under me, as I swayed back and forth, alternately relieving the pressure on each ankle. While Joe watched his train circle, I stared at all the shiny, distorted Amys reflected in the glass ornaments hanging from the tree, their bodies stretched and wrapping around their spheres like mischievous pendulums, their faces wide and short.

That Joe had not sent me angrily to bed was sheer luck, but I was all too happy to risk it. Somehow, I sensed that he wanted me to stay with him, just the two of us, alone with our separate thoughts. Around us, the house was quiet.

The silence was broken when he cleared his throat. He asked, "Do you want to try it?"

I nodded.

He scooted over so I could put my hand on the control switch. He warned me not to touch it when the train was anywhere near it, as doing so would flip the train over. There was no mistake about the horror of such an accident or about the importance of doing it just right on this one time that he let me.

The metal felt cold and rough in my hands, and I could feel the tremor of the train coming through the steel tracks.

"Now!" he urged.

I turned the knob, my whole body trembling nervously. The track switched, and the train turned sharply in my direction.

Joe and I looked into each other's eyes. The charm of this family heirloom passed between us, one generation to another, rust and all.

He watched me run the train for a long time. It was fun to play with, but what I loved most was feeling honored and connected to him. I would have eaten worms soaked in mud to get that kind of attention, anytime.

After a while, from the side, I could see his face had softened. He did not look at me, although I laid my hand on his shoulder. I slid my body a few inches back from the transformer, but he did not reach for it, even though the train was coming back around.

Hesitantly, I asked, "Are you okay?"

Joey said nothing; he just looked at me. His eyes were wet. And I knew. I understood what he was thinking, what he was feeling.

He wished I were one of his daughters or his son. But I could understand that; anyone could. He missed them every day of his life, but especially on a day like this. He wanted to see them scrambling about the house, looking for something shiny to put on the tree. He wanted to hear them bickering about whose turn it would be next. He wanted to smell their hair, freshly shampooed or caked with dirt. He wanted it so badly that it was hard to feel anything else, even at a time like this.

I, too, wished sometimes that he were my real dad instead. I wished my dad would walk in the door at that very moment and say, "My turn." He'd have a go at the train, and then he would take me to a restaurant and let me eat only dessert. Afterward, we would go to the playground I had once wanted him to see, but when we got there, I would feel embarrassed, because now I felt too old to have him push me in the swing.

Joe reached out and tenderly straightened a piece of my hair that had fallen into my mouth, waking me from my reverie. He kissed me goodnight, and I went to bed.

Throughout the years, the pain we each felt at having lost what's most precious—my "real" dad, his "real" children—was a familiar touchstone for Joe and me. Most of the time, we managed our respective heartbreak, but those moments when we felt especially close to one another made our hearts hurt fresh. So we made the best of it, deriving small comfort from shared joys, reliable and true as that old tin train, going around and around.

—*Amy Harold*

# Even as He Gives His Daughter's Hand

I have my father's hands. Short and stubby, they're not the musician's friends we both yearn for them to be.

I also studied those hands as a child. In church I'd fight to sit next to Dad, just to hold his hand. He knew I did this so I could sneak looks at the time on his watch. As I watched the minute hand chip away those Sunday hours, I also met my father in the cracks of his hands. They're slightly callused from years of providing, but they are as gentle as his spirit. He's a blue collar worker with an artist's soul. A dreamer who lives in possibility. And it is my father's hand that I held throughout my childhood—at sporting events, at doctor's offices, at the mall, and while strolling down the street.

We're lefties, my dad and me. I'm reminded of this by his lifelong quest to find the perfect pen.

Although I'm convinced he enjoys the search more than the pens themselves, I humor him and his analysis of the inadequacies of each pen.

"Oh, let's just look here, down this aisle," he'll say as he takes the shopping cart from me.

"Dad, you have tubs and tubs of pens at home," I'll respond.

"I know, but they smear all over my hand when I write. I just need to find the perfect one."

I gave up reminding him that smearing happens as a result of his left handedness, not because of a deficiency in the pens.

Pens are not the only thing my father collects. He collects leather bags and coats, guitars, more music CDs than he could ever listen to, and although his grocery cart remains sparse in the supermarket, he can easily fill it in the bookstore. Yes, he collects hobbies, and does it all with champagne taste and a beer wallet.

My father is more interested in his dogs and cars than in deciding on the right woman. He's also a brilliant and creative man who just can't find his artistic outlet. He'll never stop trying, though.

"If it weren't for bad luck, I'd have no luck at all," he says.

There is one place, though, where he knows he belongs: my dad loves fatherhood. He takes pride in being a nurturer. For that, I am grateful.

I was a bed wetter as a child. I never cried about it or even felt ashamed. I didn't have to; I had Dad.

"Dad," I'd whisper as I grabbed his hand and shook him. "Are you awake?"

"I am now," he'd whisper back.

"I think I wet my bed," I'd confess.

"Alright," he'd say, as if it were no big deal. "Let's get you cleaned up and back to bed."

What I remember most about those early-morning moments is his tenderness—and his feet. He never walked in the middle of the night; he shuffled. He shuffled as he threw dirty sheets into the washing machine, and then he shuffled upstairs to remake my bed. He shuffled through these midnight changes often and never mentioned them in the morning.

Dad is not into grandiose acts of love. It's the little, daily things that make him so special. He once drove through a tornado to pick me up from my adventures abroad. He did this in order to bring me what I'd craved while overseas: Hamburger Helper. He also drove to my college dorm late one night to deliver forty dollars. This was done in response to a phone call from me, crying because I'd run out of toothpaste and had no money to buy more. My dad did a lot of driving for me.

According to him, his aren't the only famous hands in the family. When I was young, he paid me to rub his back. He says I have "the touch." I didn't know what that meant at the time; I mostly wanted to spend time with him and the dollar he would sometimes pay me. Now, I know "the touch" means to nurture, the ability and desire to administer tender loving care, the parts of himself he sees in me.

When I first met the man who would become my husband, I saw in him a glimmer of the dreamer whose hand I'd held as a girl. Soon after this wonderful man became my fiancé, we learned that he was in dire need of a life-threatening surgery. Dad was my first call.

"Well," he said, pausing slightly. "This is a good thing. At least you know now, when it can still be fixed, before something happens. This is a good thing, a good thing."

"I just don't know what to do," I sobbed into the phone. "I can't do this."

"Well, Holly, now you have to."

My fiancé and I decided to move our wedding up and get married within the week, before the surgery. Dad showed up with a new suit and his credit card.

When surgery day arrived, so did my dad. He came before all the others and stayed after they'd all gone. He even accompanied me to my hotel and stayed there himself, "just in case." He was standing next to me when I used my married name for the first time.

"Reservations for Rutchik," I told the front desk clerk. "Oh, yes—Rutchik," the clerk said. "Two rooms under this name?"

"No," Dad said. "One for Rutchik, one for Knutson."

That's when it hit me: I was now an adult. I had a husband, a health crisis, and my own hotel room booked under my own name, a name different from my father's.

A few months later, my husband and I had the big wedding we'd planned. While on the dance floor, a friend of my dad's approached me.

"Your dad's so happy for you!" she told me. "But he's so worried you're not going to need him anymore."

"Well, all little girls grow up," I replied as I laughed and danced away.

Soon after, I fell on that dance floor and broke my leg. My new husband rushed to my side, grabbing my hand to comfort me. Within seconds, my other hand was in my dad's. As I lay on the floor in my wedding gown, grasping the hands of the only two men I'd ever loved, I realized that Dad and I were both wrong: This little girl will never grow up. I'll always need my dad's hand to hold.

—*Holly Rutchik*

# Caught in Flight

The unorthodox way in which our firstborn revealed her impending incarnation to my husband and me showed us that the depths of bonding between a dad and daughter aren't restricted to any time or place.

Before our marriage, my husband Jim and I discussed lifetime goals, hopes, and values, including children. At that time, I explained that while a student at the University of Wisconsin I had participated in a university endocrine research project. Although progesterone treatments had resolved my problem, I had been told there were no guarantees that I could conceive children. Jim assured me that if we couldn't have our own biological children we would adopt.

Still young, in love, and building careers, we were confident that when the time was right God would ensure we had children. We didn't address the problem again until the night I awoke to hear Jim mumbling in his sleep. As I lay quietly trying to decipher his words, he suddenly sprang from bed, fell to his knees, reached up and embraced air as if he'd just caught something of great value.

"Honey, what are you doing?" I asked.

"It's okay," he answered. "I caught her."

"Caught who?"

He scooped a bundle of air and embraced it to his heart. "Our daughter."

"What daughter?"

"I dreamed we were going to have a little girl. To prove I wanted her, I had to catch her before she fell."

He rose to his feet, kissed the bundle of air, and tenderly laid it beside me before sliding into bed. Without any further explanation, he fell fast asleep.

Bewildered, I lay awake, listening to his even, deep breathing, wondering what had prompted his bizarre behavior. Was his desire for fatherhood bothering him so much that he dreamt about it?

That autumn, a gynecologist confirmed that I was pregnant. We were elated.

Jim was on out-of-town business when labor pains warned me to rush to the hospital. A few hours later, our healthy, beautiful daughter was born. We named her Kathy and bonded with her immediately.

Whenever Jim cradled her in his arms, she gurgled approval and his eyes glistened with joy.

By the time Kathy sat up, he was singing and reading to her. He taught her how to ride her bicycle, to stay upright on ice skates and roller skates, to shoot baskets, to throw and catch footballs, to bat and pitch baseballs, and to swim, dive, and camp. When she became a teenager, he taught her how to drive our car.

He cried over the premature birth and death of Kathy's brother and rejoiced over the birth of her younger sister. Fatherhood was so important to Jim that he scheduled appointments so he could attend most of Kathy's school and church functions. He seldom missed her concerts or school plays, PTA meetings or teachers' conferences, and never missed Kathy quarterback in Powder Puff football games. Often, he was the only father at midday events.

As Kathy grew, she looked forward to Daddy's one-on-one milk and cookie chats before bedtime. During these conversations, when Kathy expressed her weals and woes, Jim praised her accomplishments and suggested solutions to her problems.

After college, Kathy flew the skies as a flight attendant, frequently phoning from faraway cities during her layovers. Jim was tickled when she served us on airline flights, and he was thrilled when he walked her down the aisle at her wedding.

The bond between Kathy and her dad increased over the years. One of the most ethereal events occurred during a mysterious illness that resulted in Jim being hospitalized. Kathy flew home to Colorado from Seattle. Together, we entered Jim's hospital room to find his doctor bending over his bed.

"He's not responding to treatment," the doctor acknowledged us with grim concern.

Kathy rushed to her dad's bedside, clasped his hand, and squeezed it gently. "Daddy, it's your daughter, Kathy." She kissed his forehead. "I love you."

Jim opened his eyes and in a faint voice said, "I love you, too, Kathy." Then he drifted back to sleep, leaving us anxious yet relieved that he'd recognized her.

The next morning when we entered his hospital room, Jim was sitting up in bed, flashing a smile. Eagerly, he shared his miraculous experience with us.

"I felt my life ebbing away and sensed I was drifting in the tunnel of transition, heading for the light. Then, I heard Kathy's voice and felt her kiss my forehead. When she squeezed my hand, I remembered that long-ago dream in which a voice told me that if I wanted to be a father I needed to catch my baby before she fell. I caught Kathy then. This time, Kathy caught me."

—*Sally Kelly-Engeman*

# Missing the Game and Other Father's Day Observations

Father's Day has been a most transitional holiday for me. It's not because the date changes from year to year to coincide with the second Sunday in June. It doesn't really matter *when* it is; what I'm talking about is *what* it is. Or, more precisely, what Father's Day has meant to me at different phases of my life.

As a child, Father's Day was the day when we all did whatever Dad wanted to do. All Dad ever really wanted to do was to be allowed to watch the ball game in peace and eat something he liked. So, come Father's Day, as usual, we did what Mom wanted: Under the guise of "Dad's special day," we'd go out to eat and miss the game. We'd go to any place he chose, which was always Mom's favorite place, and at the end of it all, he'd pay. He'd get presents, too. Shirts and books were always popular, since Dad read and wore clothes. I'd make a homemade card proclaiming "You are the bestest dad in the whole world!" And he'd make me feel as if it was the single greatest thing that anyone had ever done for him. At day's end, he would thank all of us for our generosity, and we'd tell him how much we loved him. We'd put that Father's Day in the books and forget about it for another year.

Things change. As a teenager, I vaguely remember blowing through whatever Father's Day gaiety was had in a hurry to get to whatever it was that I really wanted to be doing on that Sunday. I no longer made him cards and rarely remembered to buy one. Typically, I would use one that my mother had lying around and was blank inside—you know the kind, those non–holiday-specific cards with a puppy on the front—and write my sentiments on the inside. At that point, I knew better than to write "bestest," although my dad would have probably gotten a kick out of that. By then, my siblings were married and gone, and for them Father's Day was the mailing of a card and a gift. Usually a shirt or a book.

I would come home that evening from whatever it was that had occupied my time, say "Happy Father's Day, Dad," and hear him say, "Thanks, honey," as I was passing through the television room on the way to my room, where I'd stay for the balance of the night.

Things change. I got married, and the love of my life happened to have two young boys of her own.

Insta-family! I adopted them in late October of the next year. Voila! Insta-Dad! Soon, we had another child, a daughter, and I became a biological father.

So what did I learn during those early years of fatherhood? Parenting is really hard! I also started to appreciate my own father's unbelievable patience.

The meaning of Father's Day had multiplied for me—now that I was both the son of a father and a father myself. Now, I was the one getting the attention on Father's Day. I got homemade cards. I got shirts. I got books. Now, Dad and I shared something. Actually, he and I shared two things, since I was born on his birthday. But now we shared fatherhood, too; we were members of that very special fraternity. Don't get me wrong; I was always close to my Dad. We always had a lot to talk about—baseball, books, comedies . . . and now his grandchildren. My children!

Dad and I shared a few Father's Days in which we all went out to dinner and he and I missed the game together.

Things change. Dad died last June, five days before Father's Day, thirteen days before our shared birthday. Two days after Dad died, my daughter, our baby, delivered her first child and our second grandchild. The wheel of life goes round and round. So Father's Day last year was a day of overwhelming emotions. I missed Dad dearly, and I wished to have the chance to tell him again that I thought he was the bestest dad in the whole world. There was a new father in the family, too. My son-in-law was the proud daddy of a beautiful baby boy, and now it was my job to welcome him to the fatherhood fraternity.

This year, Father's Day was a time to mourn and a time to celebrate. A time to thank God for my father and to treasure all those great memories of Father's Day past. A time to enjoy and appreciate my son-in-law as he carries on the traditions—like missing the game.

Father's Day is approaching again, and I know that I will miss my Dad. I will take this special day to remember and to be grateful for him. I will also spend part of this Father's Day appreciating the father that my son-in-law is becoming. I will enjoy watching him play with his son . . . instead of watching the game.

I've seen Father's Day from all sides now. I remember sitting on my father's lap. I remember my kids sitting on my lap. Now, my grandkids sit on my lap and I watch them sit on my children's laps.

No matter how you look at it, if you are lucky enough to have kids who appreciate and love you, every day is Father's Day. And if your dad is with my dad, I hope they are watching the game.

*—Jon Sherman*

# Across the Miles

As a nine-year-old only child, I assumed my world would always be a peaceful, happy place. Then, one sunny Saturday morning, my parents dissolved my illusions with their simple announcement: they were getting a divorce.

Change stormed my life like an angry tornado, uprooting everything I had known. Dad moved out. Mom remarried. We moved—twice. Dad remarried. Soon he and my stepmom, Karen, were expecting a baby. By age thirteen, I was staring into the eyes of my brand-new baby half-brother, Dylan. It was hard to tell which of us was more dazed by the experience. Within a few days of Dylan's birth, Dad left for New York; his new family soon followed, while I stayed in Oregon with my mom and stepdad.

As I struggled through my teenage years, my relationship with my father grew distant. We talked on the phone and saw each other occasionally, but I never felt he and my stepmom really knew me or understood me. I thought attending Syracuse University, where my dad and Karen were both professors, would change that. Instead, I was given more space than I expected, and when we did get together, the close, familial intimacy I had naively anticipated did not materialize. I felt warmly welcomed but not like I fit in. True connection requires more than the occasional enchilada night, I learned.

After my college graduation, I left town and got a job, and at age twenty-four, I married. I moved a few times, ultimately ending up back in Oregon. Telephone conversations with my dad were sporadic. I missed him and wished we talked more, but I stayed ridiculously stubborn: He practically never called me, so why should I call him? Like a spurned teenage girl, I inflicted the silent treatment on a guy who had no idea he was receiving it.

At age twenty-eight, I had a change of heart. I made a New Year's resolution to call my dad every month and rebuild our relationship. In the beginning, it was extremely hard for me to pick up the phone. With each call I initiated, I had to swallow my pride and convince myself it wasn't foolish and egocentric to think he'd want to hear from me. I kept at it, anyway, and after many months, I noticed something: he had started calling me, too.

The more we spoke, the more we connected. Our talks reminded us that we are strikingly similar people, sharing not only a mutual appreciation for writing, the Oregon coast, and bad puns, but also a set of attitudes, core beliefs, and philosophies. As our relationship deepened, I began to feel I was more than the remnant of his past that I had sometimes feared I was. I began to believe in us.

About two weeks before my thirtieth birthday, which fell on a Sunday, my father called from New York to tell me he was having a present delivered to me the Monday before my birthday. I was curious, but I didn't pressure him for details; I like to be surprised.

A couple of days later, my husband Frank asked me if I intended to go to the gym after work that Monday.

"Yeah, why?" I said, focused on something else.

"Well, your dad said you needed to be home when the gift arrived."

I stopped and looked at him. "I have to sign for something?"

"I guess," he shrugged. "He just said it was going to be delivered in the evening, and you should be there when it came."

That night, a Thursday, I lay awake in bed, my mind spinning. *What delivery company comes during the evening? Don't they only deliver from eight to five? Why did I have to be home that night?*

I thought about Saturday, the day Frank and I had planned a major spring cleaning. My pile-loving husband had suggested that the two of us take on this cleaning extravaganza (suspicious fact number one), and he had scheduled the date for it two months in advance (suspicious fact number two). I had wondered at the time what had possessed him to pick that random Saturday in April to overhaul our apartment, and now I thought I knew: the Monday delivery had to be a surprise visit from my father.

I was awake for hours with excitement, piecing together the puzzle. *Why else would I get my gift in the evening, when I had to be home for it? Why else would Frank mysteriously insist we clean the house that particular weekend? Dad, Karen, and Dylan were about to visit us—that had to be why!* It had been about three years since I'd seen them. We'd been in New York for only a few days. My brother had been thirteen then.

Once the idea entered my head, I was obsessed. The suspense was more agonizing than any I had ever experienced; it was a painful, desperate kind that I didn't think I could survive. I couldn't sleep, and my stomach was in a perpetual knot. By Saturday night, Frank found me crying in the bedroom.

He sat down next to me on the bed and put his arm around me. "What's wrong?" he asked.

"The surprise . . ." I said, fighting to get words out through my tears. "I want it to be my dad. I miss him so much."

The birthday present I wanted, more than any other present I'd ever wished for, was to see my father. I cried hard, struggling with an unexpected avalanche of emotion. Subconsciously, I had refused to let myself miss him. Now that we might actually be together, I was suffocating on my hope.

"I know, honey," Frank said, holding me. "I miss my family too."

By the time Monday afternoon dragged into place, I was still ricocheting between the certainty that my father was going to walk through my front door that night and the belief that my suspicions were nothing more than wishful thinking. I went to the gym early and made myself exercise. Then I went home, showered, dressed, and sat nervously on the couch—back straight, eyes vacant, perched as if waiting for someone to take my picture.

"I have a surprise," Frank said from the kitchen.

That perked me up. Frank had admitted earlier

that he knew what the mystery gift would be, but he wasn't telling. Maybe now he'd tell me.

"I got us salmon for dinner," he continued, unloading the groceries he'd just brought in. "I figured you might need some cheering up."

My heart sank. Maybe my hopes were just that—hopes, not reality. My anticipation deflated completely when Frank started cooking.

"Aren't you going to wait?" I asked feebly.

"For what?" he said, putting butter in a skillet.

"You know . . ." I mumbled, "in case we have company."

Before he could respond, the phone rang. I rushed to the study and answered with an anxious hello.

"Did it get there yet?" my father asked.

"No. I've been waiting, but nothing yet."

"It should have been there by now," he said, a frown in his voice. "Just check the front porch for me, okay? I'll hold on the line."

"Okay," I said, feeling anticipation grip my stomach.

I put the phone down, ran into the living room, and yanked open the front door.

There, standing rakishly before me, legs crossed at the ankles, left palm leaning casually against the doorframe, was a handsome teenage guy about six feet tall. Blue eyes, blond hair, great smile. My brother!

I jumped into his arms and started crying. I saw my father standing off to the side, holding his cell phone and jokingly still talking into the now-forgotten phone line. I let Dylan get some air back into his lungs and turned to enfold my father in the biggest bear hug I could give. It was a good five minutes before I could stop sniffling with joy and relief.

We spent the week together at a resort hotel along the Oregon coast. I missed seeing Karen, my stepmom, but I was grateful for what they had decided they could afford: one brother, one father, and one week of precious free time. I got to know my brother better; this nearly seventeen-year-old young man was a different person than he had been when we'd last seen each other, and I really enjoyed "meeting" him. Best of all, my dad and I took long walks on the beach together and shared plenty of heartfelt talks, warm hugs, and pints of gourmet chocolate ice cream.

I took pictures throughout our visit, and after the trip was over, I matted four of the best photos together in a large frame. The pictures show us with genuine, goofy-with-happiness grins that reflect our delight in finally being in each other's company. It makes me sad to think that it took me so many years to put aside my pride and fear and to reach out. I had to go first, to be the one to say, "I want us to be closer"—but that doesn't matter to me anymore. I look at that collage of memories and see the best, most meaningful birthday gift I've ever received.

I wanted my father to remember, too, so for Father's Day I sent him a framed collage of the same pictures. It makes me smile to think that, each time I stop to appreciate my photos, nearly 3,000 miles away, my dad might be looking at them and thinking about me, too.

*—Alaina Smith*

# The Fruit of
# a Man's Life

It was just a silly little pear tree that he planted for me. At least that's what I thought when I was eight. I mean, it looked like any other tree, basically, just kind of leafy green. And, anyway, it never produced any pears.

I guess my dad didn't feel the same way about "my" pear tree, because every morning from out my bedroom window I saw him in his overalls on bended knees, swishing dirt around the pear tree and then giving it a huge bath. He would check every single leaf, kind of the same way the safety monitor checked on each one of us kids before we stepped on the school bus. And I'm not really sure about this part, but I think he talked to that silly little tree, because I used to see his lips moving a lot. I could never really be sure, though, and I surely wasn't going to ask him, because I definitely didn't want to grow up knowing I had a Dad who talked to trees.

By the time I finished my morning cereal, he was always heading back in through the screened porch door with about the same kind of look on his face that my teacher Miss Stevens had when she told us she was getting married. I didn't actually know what grown-ups were thinking about when they made those doofy-looking faces, but they sure looked happy.

Twenty-three summers and two colleges came and went, and there sat that silly old pear tree, still without any pears, I might add.

On my way to work one morning I stopped by my parents' house and spotted my dad through the family room window poking the ground around the pear tree with his cane. He smiled big when he saw me, as he always did. I smiled back big too. Curious, I went outside and asked Dad why a man would spend over thirty years' worth of mornings tending to a silly old pear tree that never even returned the promised fruit.

His words are as vivid today as in that moment when he muttered them softly with his head held high.

"The reward is not the pear itself, but rather the journey a man is willing to make in the hope of one day finding a pear."

Unfortunately, back then, I thought he was trying to sound like the new Shakespeare, so I ignored the statement. Privately, though, I kept trying to figure out what the heck he meant. He passed away before I could ask him.

The years passed, and I married and moved away from my hometown. My widowed mother remained in my childhood home.

During a visit back home many years after that conversation with my dad, my stepdaughter and I were walking outside together when I spotted the pear tree. I explained to her that my dad had planted the pear tree for me when I was exactly her age.

She wasn't at all impressed and told me it looked like a silly tree, and besides, it had no pears.

I was about to explain to her that the pears weren't really what mattered, that the journey is what mattered most. But before I could, the epiphany hit, and I finally understood my dad's words of so long ago. Looking up toward the sky, I smiled and gave the thumbs-up sign.

Glancing down at the base of the pear tree just as we were leaving, I noticed a piece of folded foil peeking up from the dirt. Inside, wrapped in a piece of weathered plastic, was a photograph of a pear that had been meticulously cut out from a magazine.

The inscription at the bottom was written by a very familiar gardener's hands:

> *"A man's life, if spent in hopeful tending, yields far more than the promised fruit could ever bear."*

I was reminded once again of the new Shakespeare, but this time I understood immediately.

Coworkers often ask the significance of the framed picture of the pear on my desk. I can only manage to say that my dad planted a tree for me when I was very young and it bore its first real fruit once I became old.

—*Lisa Leshaw*

# Act of Atonement

The smallest, meanest thing I've ever done, I did to my father. At twenty-one, though I still lived at home, I had just landed my first "important" job. A couple of new friends from work—sophisticated, successful women in my eyes—invited me to lunch, and I wanted to make a good impression.

Dad called the office after we left and learned of our plans. I felt sure that my companions' fathers were professional people. When I saw Dad, dressed in a working man's clean but well-worn clothing, peering through the restaurant window that day, I was ashamed of him. I hid behind a pillar so I wouldn't have to acknowledge him as my father.

One of the women asked if I knew that funny little man who seemed to be trying to find someone, and I replied, "Of course not." He finally went away.

That evening Dad said he was sorry he'd missed the chance to buy lunch for my friends and me. I pray that he never knew the truth.

I'll be ashamed of what I did that day for the rest of my life. It haunts me more than other, worse mistakes I've made, because the snub was so undeserved and I was so wrong about what mattered. It's too late to go back and proudly present my father to my friends. The only act of atonement I know how to make is to introduce you now to my father.

Dad was a gentle man who expected the best of each morning. Simple things pleased him most: the coming of summer, when he could smell the roses and taste the melons and tomatoes he had planted in the earth; a ragtag little dog named Dusty, who was always within petting distance; and sitting on a river bank, hoping to catch a fish.

When I was little and awoke from a bad dream, he'd hold me on his lap and tell me a story, and I wasn't afraid anymore. If something was important to me, it mattered to him, too. He shared my small victories, and his heart wept my tears.

Dad paid his bills and kept his promises and refused to take the easy way if it compromised his principles. I still recall his lovely laugh.

At times, I could have strangled him. When the "shortcuts" he insisted on taking led ever farther from our destination, he drove stubbornly on, refusing to stop for directions or even to admit we were lost.

He loved a good cigar. Though liquor had no place in our Baptist household, he and Mom would sometimes open a bottle of Mogen David wine during the holidays and giggle at one another like two naughty children.

The ability to trust others was one of Dad's greatest talents. His faith in people was so strong that they sometimes surprised themselves by becoming what he'd always believed them to be.

With all his heart he was a Christian, and he remained convinced throughout his lifetime that those who love God and their fellow man can come to no lasting harm.

Holidays were his favorite time, to be celebrated with unrestrained pleasure. He strung red bells and silver tinsel all over the house at Christmas, filled a tub with apples for Halloween bobbing, and decorated each egg at Easter as if it were a work of art.

His poetry praised the things he loved: the beauty of the earth, music, and my mother. Piano lessons were a luxury beyond his reach, but his hands moved swiftly over the keys of our old Steinway, playing by ear the songs he sang with such gusto: "Redwing,"

"Turkey in the Straw," "The Old Rugged Cross." Sundays found him at his regular spot in the tenor section of our church choir.

Dad dreamed many dreams, but few came true. Still, the failure of one plan never diminished his enthusiasm for the next.

When the economy was in trouble, Dad decided there was big money to be made in tree trimming. Don't ask me why. He said something about the fact that no one was taking care of their trees properly, which created an obvious need. Undeterred by the fact that he knew nothing about tree trimming, Dad said, "How hard could it be? All you do is climb a tree and saw off a dead limb." He painted a large sign and drove around town advertising his services. Mother was terrified that he would fall from a tree and break his neck. She needn't have worried. I don't think he found enough customers to pay for the big sign.

Next, he decided he could make money growing and selling sweet potatoes. He rented a small piece of land and planted his crop. He loved watching them grow, and each weekend, he went to tend them. Finally, he announced it was time to dig them up and sell his crop. His excitement infected us all. Grandma promised him a sweet potato pie. Shortly after he left, he returned home; someone had already dug up his sweet potatoes and left only empty land. Mother went over and hugged him.

A couple of days later, Dad said, "You know, I've been thinking, a fella has to be pretty desperate to dig up another man's sweet potatoes. I bet that's all he had to feed his family. So maybe he needed them a whole lot worse than we did."

Dad's most enduring dream began even before he and Mom were married. He was working at whatever jobs he could find around west Texas. People in the tiny town of Channing were excited; word was the railroad was coming through. Everybody thought that meant the price of land would shoot sky-high. Dad saved and scraped together enough money to buy a small plot that he hoped might serve as a nest egg for the family he would have one day. He held on to that dusty little scrap of prairie for the rest of his life. The railroad never came through, and after Dad's death, I sold the land for $150, which I donated in his name to the Humane Society. My kind father would have liked that. Maybe the money would help save a dog that would bring years of happiness to someone.

Dad's kindness was remarkable. To Mom's dismay, the barber who cut Dad's hair butchered it. But Dad refused to take his business elsewhere, because the old gentleman had few remaining customers and needed the work.

It was Dad who taught me to waltz, when I was twelve, at the family dances held in McKinley Park. He read to me until I could read for myself. When my pet frog died, he helped me bury it beneath a pile of pure white pebbles.

The prettiest dress I ever owned was a rare, store-bought gift from my father. To an objective observer that day, I would have appeared gangly, an unformed fourteen-year-old. But when I stepped tentatively from the store's dressing room in softest velvet, through Dad's eyes I first saw myself as beautiful.

When Dad died, the church overflowed. It would have astonished him to learn that so many people grieved.

The facts of his life are these: His mother, who had ten children, died soon after his birth. At the age of seven, he traveled with his father and brothers across Oklahoma in a covered wagon, laying ties for the railroad. His family couldn't afford to send him to school after the eighth grade, so his dream of becoming a minister died early. A picture of him, taken during World War I, shows a vulnerable-looking seventeen-year-old, with a crew cut, staring solemnly into the camera. His marriage to my mother lasted thirty-seven years, and after her death, I found tender love notes he had written to her throughout his lifetime. Most of his jobs were mundane ones—grocery clerk, Pullman conductor—but he always gave his best. My folks had their own grocery once, but they lost it during the Depression, when they wouldn't withhold the food on their shelves from hungry customers who couldn't pay.

Forgive me, Dad, for that day so long ago when I denied that I knew you. Today, you are the standard by which I measure my life. Once, you told me I was your life's miracle; I know now that having you as my father was mine.

—*Ramona John*

*A version of this story was first published in the Salvation Army's* War Cry, *July 7, 2001.*

# Tale of a Kite
# Without a Tail

"The wind is fast," the little girl announced excitedly, half out of breath from racing inside and upstairs. "Can we fly my kite?"

The little girl had gotten her very first kite a few weeks before and had patiently waited for an afternoon that wasn't too calm or too rainy or too windy. This day, she hoped, like Little Bear's porridge, was "just right."

The father looked at the treetops dancing in the breeze. "Go get your kite," he said, smiling.

Hand in hand, they walked to the park, the blonde little girl pretty in pink and as excited as if she were coming down the stairs on Christmas morning.

The little girl's kite cost all of ninety-nine cents (with a spool of cotton string included in the bargain), but it had something the more expensive models did not: a rainbow on its plastic skin. The little girl, you should know, dearly loves rainbows.

Kites of paper, like those the father used to fly when he was the little girl's age—"three, almost four"—are impossible to find nowadays, as are kites shaped like kites ought to be shaped, that is, like a diamond, taller than wide. The little girl's kite was wider than tall, like an eagle with wings spread.

"Let's go fly a kite . . ." sang the little girl, now skipping and wearing her father's too-large-for-her "Johnny Bench hat," as she calls his Cincinnati Reds baseball cap. ". . . Up to the highest height . . ."

When the kite was soaring up where the air is clear, the father let the little girl take hold of the string.

"Wow! Neat! Cool!"

The little girl was also excited.

"It feels like catching a big fish in the sky," she said, a wonderful observation considering the little girl has never felt the tug of a fish. (Her father, unfortunately, rarely feels the tug of a fish, either, though not for lack of trying.)

Then . . . the kite took a nosedive and crashed to earth like a kamikaze going down a ship's smokestack. Fortunately, it escaped damage.

The little girl sprinted to the fallen kite as if an Olympic gold medal were at stake, picked it up, and counted "One-two-three!" before letting go as the father pulled on the string. The kite again quickly soared up to the highest height.

Then another kamikaze crash. And another Olympic sprint. And "One-two-three!" And again the rainbow kite soared up where the air is clear before crashing once more.

"Your kite needs a tail," the father remarked.

"A tail?" the little girl echoed quizzically, rolling her eyes and giggling. "Daddy, you bingo-bum (her own made-up word for a silly person). Kites don't have tails—doggies and kitty cats and monkeys have tails."

The father laughed and tried to explain that in the "old days" you tied strips of cloth together to make a tail, which kept the kite upright and prevented it from crashing. He also warned that you must always make sure to use old rags, telling her about the time, when he was a little boy, that he got in trouble for cutting up one of his dad's—uh, Grandpa's—good shirts to use as a tail.

This, of course, made the little girl laugh even more—the idea of her daddy being scolded by Gramps.

With no rags handy, they sent the tail-less rainbow kite soaring as high as a rainbow.

*Snap!*

The cheap cotton string broke, and the kite fluttered away over a row of tall trees.

"Oh no!" the little girl cried out. "It's going into The Gully!"

Hand in hand, the father and little girl hurried to the edge of The Gully and spotted the kite far below, high up in a tree.

The father helped the little girl climb through a gate with a NO TRESPASSING sign posted on it. At the risk of a $500 fine, he was going to get back her 99-cent rainbow.

The father climbed the tree (When was the last time he had done that? Ten years ago? Fifteen, maybe?) and rescued the little girl's very first kite and a small piece of his own childhood in the process.

"Thank you, Daddy," the little girl said happily and sweetly, giving a tight hug and a kiss as reward. Then, examining the broken string, she added, "I think we need a stronger rope."

The very next day, the two went to a kite store to get a stronger "rope."

"That's a pretty one," the little girl said gleefully, surveying a blue and red, state-of-the-art nylon kite that was nearly as big as a hang glider. "But I like mine better."

The father looked at the price tag: $120! There were also kites for $90 and $49 and $21. But there were no 99-cent kites. No paper kites that need rag tails. No kites shaped like kites ought to be shaped, like diamonds, taller than wide. And, fortunately, none the little girl liked better than her rainbow kite.

She did find the "rope" she wanted: 500 feet of nylon string on a plastic yellow spool. Five dollars of "rope" for a 99-cent kite, but the father did not mind in the least.

At the cashier's counter, she changed her mind, for that's a little woman's prerogative too.

"I think I want the blue one," she said and skipped off to get the "rope" on a blue spool.

As they were walking hand-in-hand out of the store, the little girl studied all the many kites on display, all of them tailless. Suddenly, she stopped abruptly and looked up at her father.

"Daddy, you bingo-bum!" she giggled. "I told you kites don't have tails. Only animals do."

—*Woody Woodburn*

# Legacy of Laughter

Laughing is one of the things my father does best. His blue eyes twinkle without even trying. When he really laughs, he bends slightly forward at the waist and braces himself with one arm against the nearest wall or cupboard, surrendering to an infectious joy that rumbles up from his toes.

At seventy-five, Dad still enjoys *Bugs Bunny* and *Roadrunner* cartoons. He's able to find humor in almost everything.

When his farm dog's tail got caught between a pulley and belt on a small feed mill, bringing everything to a dramatic halt, he laughed. When a baby owl found its way down the chimney one night and was discovered blinking sleepily behind an arm chair in the morning, he laughed. When I caught him standing beside the shower in the basement with the water running in an attempt to fool my mother into thinking he was scrubbing away a day's worth of grime, we both laughed hysterically. That infamous incident is now referred to as "passing through the mist."

"Take a shower and don't pass through the mist," my mother says bossily when he comes in smelling of the barn.

My dad's quirky sense of humor can raise my mother's ire. An acquaintance shared that her husband had passed away, and my dad, awkward and unsure how to handle the news, laughed. My mother was horrified. Later, she gave him a stern lecture on the inappropriateness of laughing when someone dies. Apparently, however, that lesson was quickly forgotten. Several months later, a neighbor related his dog's demise beneath the tires of a tractor, and my dad laughed.

My mother, who is the serious one, likes to remind us about the time she came home from grocery shopping and found me asleep in my crib with my shoes on. My dad was babysitting, and at nap time, he buttoned sleepers over my white leather baby shoes and carefully tucked me under the blankets.

"Of all things," she tsks, shaking her head while my father and I look at each other and laugh.

For years, my father and I have pulled pranks on each other—much to my mother's chagrin. "The

Letter" has become as legendary as Passing Through The Mist.

Posing as the president of an automobile company, I wrote to my dad, inventing mechanical malfunctions with his new car. In official-sounding terms, I outlined why the tires, windshield wipers, exhaust system, and seat belts were defective and would result in the recall of his vehicle.

My dad called the dealership. The manager was stumped and called the president. No one understood the technical terminology or knew what to do. It was during a third telephone conversation with the dealership that it dawned on my father that he'd been had. He told me later as we both held our sides laughing that he said to the flummoxed manager, "Wait a minute, I think this is my daughter's doing."

At the core of my father's buoyant spirit is an innocent, tender-hearted goodness that draws everyone to him. He's the one on the street that panhandlers target. He's the person in the room that a child is drawn to or a pet selects to curl up with. Few forget his gentleness.

Several years ago at a township meeting for landowners affected by a municipal tile drainage system, my father and a cantankerous farmer held differing views. The farmer reacted by threatening to block a section of tile that ran from his property to my father's and emptied into a creek.

Angry and hurt, my father said, "You wouldn't do that."

"Yes, I would," the farmer shot back.

An excruciating silence filled the room. My father replied quietly, "Well, I didn't know I had a neighbor like that."

At that, the meeting disintegrated, and the farmer left. He never tampered with the tile or mentioned it again.

For reasons I don't fully understand, my father views life through a lens of simple yet profound grace, a lens colored with contagious idealism and generosity, despite some of the difficult circumstances of his life.

Photographs of my father as a child reveal a pale, serious boy dressed in longish wool shorts and suspenders. My grandparents adopted him as a sickly, neglected, twelve-month-old orphan with rickets. An only child, he was raised on a farm with turkeys, pigs, peacocks, cats, go-carts, and love. My grandmother spoiled him. As youngsters, my brother and I begged for the story about the box of chocolates. Grandmother had sent them out with our dad for workers in the field, but the chocolates never arrived—he ate them all.

Dad married my mother when he was twenty-four, and several years later they took over the farm.

During my youth, I was blissfully unaware of our desperate financial situation and near-bankruptcy. My world consisted of a mother who loved me and a father who doted on me. Discipline was left to my mother; I remember my father spanking me only once, a few taps that filled me with tearful remorse.

My dad calls me "Mussy," and I call him "Mulcum." I'm not sure why the nicknames started, but they represent to me a deep, abiding delight in our relationship as father and daughter.

A German shepherd Dad once owned was so crazy about him that she used to circle the house, looking through the windows. When she spotted him, usually through the sliding glass doors in the den where he watches television, she'd sit and stare at him.

"Silly mutt of a thing," my dad would always say, chuckling affectionately.

But I understood her devotion; I feel the same way.

My father has taught me the language of laughter. And of this I'm certain: there is no finer teacher.

As an unsure sixteen-year-old taking my driver's test, I turned too sharply beside a hydro pole. I will never forget the terror in the instructor's eyes as he glimpsed the approaching pole. Finally, in desperation, he reached out and grabbed the dash, shouting, "Stop! Stop!" With typical teenage aplomb I gave my parents' Chevy Malibu Classic more gas, upon which it screeched against and around the pole and shot out into the intersection. I failed my exam. Shortly after, the instructor resigned.

My dad and I have laughed often about that humiliation and the unfortunate, battle-scarred Chevy. In his laughter I heard, "My grace to you will never run out."

Seven years ago my father's bowel ruptured and he spent a week in the hospital. Before reconstructive surgery, he was required to wear a colostomy bag. He hated its inconvenience and constant reminder of life's fragility, but when we laughed about it, I heard, "We can overcome anything because we have each other."

And when he laughs with me at some of my worst mistakes, I hear, "I'll love you always."

This beautiful language of laughter, which my father speaks so eloquently, lifts my soul. It envelops me in a warm embrace, filling all my empty nooks and crannies, soothing the frayed edges sustained by life's wear and tear, and nourishing my parched places. When we laugh together, no matter where we are, it always feels as though I'm home.

I hope it can be said of me that from my father I've learned the art of laughing well.

—*Rachel Wallace–Oberle*

# Safety Net

My dad and I can set our watches by each other. Every Tuesday and Thursday after I drive my son's carpool, I head back to the main street in our town. Rain or shine, between 8:10 and 8:15 A.M., I know I'll spot him carrying a white plastic grocery bag and wearing his large, oversized orange parka. Most days, he is plugged into his iPod; my dad is teaching himself Japanese by listening to tapes on his daily five-mile morning walks. He knows we'll run into each other, and he brings me a bag filled with articles and tidbits that he thinks would interest me. I get this plastic "life support" bag at least once a week.

When I get home, I open up the plastic bag. Each time, its content differs, but the message is the same: take care of yourself. This week there's a coupon for 50 percent off on film development, an article on breast cancer and the benefits of self-examination, an article on skin care, and vitamins. Once in a while, he finds and cuts out an article about one of my old high school classmates—getting married, receiving a promotion, moving out of town or back into town. Although there are times when I feel annoyed as I sift through the myriad small pieces of paper that I feel compelled to at least peruse, I realize this isn't about sharing pieces of paper; it's about sharing pieces of our lives.

I count on my dad being there, wearing his big, oversized orange parka and walking with the gait of a teenager. No one would believe he recently celebrated his eightieth birthday. When I pull up beside him each morning, he deftly hops in. Together, we go to Peet's or Starbucks to have a cup of coffee and a scone, but more importantly, to connect.

Today, we sit at Starbuck's talking about what each of us has planned for the day.

"I'm going to a lecture on the U.C. Berkeley campus, then over to the city. They're having the monthly brown-bag opera at the Galleria, you know," he says.

I had never realized the full life my dad was leading while I sat at work staring at my computer screen each day. I'm not sure what I thought he did, but I know I didn't think he did so much.

I ask him if we can meet again tomorrow for another cuppa joe.

"I'd love to, but I'm taking a sushi-making class," he answers. "Can we have lunch instead?"

Although our morning ritual only began when I stopped working in the city a little over a year ago, my ability to count on him has been there since I took my first breath.

As a young child, I would sit by the window staring at the street until he pulled up in his cherished 1949 Studebaker. When I was growing up, he used to spend a few hours each weekend just tinkering around with that car. He adorned it with every gizmo invented. I'm sure it was the only car around with a rear-view mirror that reflected a width of fifty yards.

"Better to be safe than sorry," he'd tell me.

I was the only one of my friends who, at age thirteen, could change a tire.

His wisdom seemed unending, as did his patience. Whenever we brought home school forms that required our parents to list their vocation, I always filled in the line entitled "Father's Occupation" myself. I loved telling my friends what he did. "My dad's a chemist," I would say, bursting with pride.

As he settles into his mug of coffee, he checks the bag I've handed him.

"You saved the *Chronicle's* pink section for me, didn't you?" he asks his usual Tuesday-morning question.

"Dad, you know I always do," I say, handing over my own sack of trivia I've gathered for him.

Each week, my bag for him contains the pink section of the newspaper (of course), some schoolwork from my son (his only grandchild), and usually a clipping of an event I think he may want to attend.

This man—who makes his own jam, takes sea-kayaking lessons, holds the anchor ropes for my son while he rock-climbs, has more volunteer hours at my son's school than I do, serves on the board of his mother's nursing home, ushers at any event he can at Zellerbach, and never misses a production of the San Francisco Opera—still makes me feels as if he has all the time in the world for me.

When I was fourteen, I joined the Girl Sea Scouts, better known as the "Mariners." It was the night before the annual Mariner's Regatta, and with a barely legible photocopy of instructions, I sat on my bed struggling to learn to tie the several types of knots our troop was to be tested on the next day. I fell apart on my bed and cried, knowing I'd never memorize all of them by morning.

That's when I heard a gentle knocking on my bedroom door.

"Linda, what's the matter?" Dad asked softly.

"I'll never remember all of this. I can't tie even one single knot," I sobbed.

"Let's just take it one step at a time," he said calmly. "Tell me what you need to know."

He stayed up with me until 2:00 A.M. that night, teaching me and testing me until I could tie all of the knots with my eyes shut.

As I emerged from childhood to adolescence, we went on countless walks together. It was on these walks that he talked to me about life and choices and consequences. All of the things I have had the courage and the strength to do in my life resulted from the belief in myself that he instilled in me. He was my biggest supporter as I was learning to fly a small plane. He and my mother were on the next available flight from their vacation in Hawaii when my husband walked out on my young son and me.

Now, as I find myself in my forties, his care and concern for me has not dissipated. If I need to make a trip, he still asks that I call when I arrive.

Although there have been countless occasions that have made me realize how special a man he is and how very lucky I am, I have never felt more proud of my dad than during the past two months when his ninety-eight-year-old mother became ill. He sat by her bedside every day, spoon-feeding her with meals he prepared himself, in an effort to keep her comfortable during her last days. He cared for her until she passed away, never showing signs of exasperation or impatience, even when the call for such human emotion was overdue. His mother taught him the power of kindness and strength, and it was only natural for him to be there for her when she needed him most. He has spent his life passing that wisdom on to me, his only child.

My father has always been, and continues to be, there for me. I live my life knowing this, taking strength from it, and believing in myself because he so deeply believes in me. He is my anchor and my safety net, and perhaps because I know he stands ready to catch, I have never been afraid to fall.

—*Linda Goldfarb*

# 29 Hours and
# 37 Minutes

This weekend my two-and-a-half-year-old daughter and I went camping for the first time. Okay, so we had running water, plenty of electricity, and lots of food. And, no, we never actually left the house. But our wilderness was no less desolate than when a lone coyote atop a hill howls over a sun-baked desert at a rising moon. Because at our "campsite," Mom was not to be found within a hundred miles.

Our circumstance was prescribed by an event that occurred on the preceding Tuesday. I had just arrived home from a long day at the office, imagining a scene in which my lovely wife, dressed in slinky evening attire, met me adoringly, holding my slippers in one hand and a fresh minty drink in the other.

When I opened the door, the living room had the decimated and ransacked appearance one expects to see in the aftermath of a hurricane, but the eerie feeling I got was of being in its eye. I carefully picked a path through the clutter of toys, books, and papers strewn everywhere until I stood in the middle of the room. Then I meekly called out, "Honey, I'm home."

"Yeah, I see," my wife said, blowing by me with a kiss that might have hit me square on the cheek had I been an extremely fat man whose face was swollen from just having his wisdom teeth removed. April was in a hot game of hide-and-seek with Kayla and obviously had not had a moment to conjure up the aforementioned minty liquid libation.

*I'll try another tack,* I thought to myself. "Sweetie, what's for dinner?"

"Whatever you brought home," came the clipped response from somewhere under the dining room table.

From her next hiding place behind the sofa, her barely audible words, "I need a break," stopped me cold. This was different from the usual, "Give me five minutes to go to the bathroom and I'm good until bedtime," or "Could you take Kayla for an hour so I can take a bath and maybe read a chapter?" It wasn't only what she said that was different, either; it was also how she'd said it. Her voice sounded guttural, thick with passion and power, dangerous, and it sent a chill down my spine that made the thinning curly hairs on the top of my head stand straight up.

Of course, that her eyes were rolled back in their sockets and her head was spinning like a carnival top were also pretty convincing evidence of a serious problem.

Clearly, I had a situation here. One that called for some fast, on-target thinking.

"Sweetheart," I said, "you need a vacation."

I saw a notable slowing of the spinning head. Seizing the opportunity, I continued.

"Maybe you could go down south and visit Stasia for a day or two."

Her hazel eyes appeared again and only one of them was still twitching uncontrollably.

So that's how the deal began, and plans were quickly made for April's impending departure to a four-star hotel, where a sauna and delicate morsels prepared by hands other than her own were waiting to be shared with a favorite cousin.

With the initial crisis abated, I had several days to prepare for my alone time with Kayla. As April's happy anticipation escalated, my nerves frayed in equal measure. Could I really survive the obvious madness I had proposed in a moment of fright? And what of Kayla's safety? Sure, I had moved from being an inexperienced wimp of a man who, a mere three years ago, had never even held a baby to a father who could wipe, cream, and powder my child's bottom faster than a short-order cook could grease the grill and crack open an egg. But parenting without a mother net? I wasn't so sure . . .

"What did you say, honey? Do I know where what's kept?"

"The syrup of ipecac," she repeated.

"No. Where?"

"The closet."

"Whose closet?"

"Our hall closet," she stated with the clear voice and patience of someone about to go on vacation.

The ipecac syrup was apparently something I should use if I needed to throw up, which is certainly what I felt like doing as Kayla and I waved goodbye to April pulling out of the driveway.

I may not have understood every little instruction I had been given, but the message of my wife's Hyundai peeling off and the smell of burning rubber were pretty clear.

"Why Mama go so fast?" Kayla asked.

"Oh, she just needs a little break, honey. She'll be back tomorrow."

Well, as the twenty-nine hours and thirty-seven minutes alone with my daughter turned out, it was neither black nor blue. There were no boo-boos that couldn't be mended with a kiss, no colored markers that didn't wash off with soap and water, and no need for ipecac syrup. Our time was filled with walks in the woods, building block castles, tea parties, a couple of Barney videos, and having a whole lot of fun together.

April returned, just like the promissory note I made her sign said she would, and she seemed relaxed and refreshed in the bargain.

I hope I'm not struck down by lightning or something for sounding cocky, but if April's head starts spinning around and her eyes roll back in her head a year or two from now, I'd be perfectly willing to do it again.

—*Samuel P. Clark*

*This story was first published in* MotherTongue, *Fall 1996, a limited-distribution periodical that has since ceased publication.*

# The Grand
# Poobah of Cars

God. Country. Family. Cars.

Those are my father's great loves, and he's suffered for each in turn. For love of God, he's lived seventy-six years as a true believer. (As a Catholic, and God knows all Catholics suffer; just ask one of us.) For love of Country, he served twenty years in the U. S. Army, including a tour in Vietnam. For love of Family, he's given fifty-five years of endless support, strength, and guidance to an unmanageable troop of wife, kids, grandkids, and now, a great-grandchild. But it is perhaps for love of Cars that the Colonel has suffered most of all. The man who lived to drive—the more powerful, challenging, and fast, faster, fastest the ride, the better—taught us all to drive. Or at least he tried to. And he bought us all cars.

My mother Marilyn was the first. A striking brunette with long, Cyd Charisse legs, Mom was a nineteen-year-old nondriver when she married Dad in 1954. The Colonel—a newly commissioned Second

Lieutenant then—believed that every grown-up should know how to drive. Especially an officer's wife, charged with tending the home fires while Daddy went off to play war games. He'd tried to teach her to drive before they were married, back home in Lafayette, Indiana. They'd used her father Joe's 1949 Chevy, whose standard transmission proved a challenge for my mother (a precursor of clutch trouble to come in future generations). Mom popped the clutch and ran the Chevy into a ditch. Dad yelled; Mom cried. The third time this happened, Joe put an end to the driving lessons.

But after they were married, Dad tried again. Mom refused. "I do not shift," my mother told my father. "I am shiftless." Dad persisted. The place was Ft. Sill, an artillery base in the middle of nowhere, Oklahoma. The car was a 1954 Dodge with one of the early two-step automatic clutches. The compromise was one that would last a lifetime: automatic transmission.

Fast forward to 1970. At fourteen, I was way too young to drive, but the state of Kansas didn't know that. In a region where there was more wheat than people, kids learned to drive tractors as toddlers, so the issuing of driver's licenses to teens who've been plowing fields for a decade didn't seem like a dangerous thing to so. But I hadn't been plowing fields since I was a toddler; I'd been playing dolls and reading books and dancing around the house to the Beatles and Simon and Garfunkel. I could ride a bike, but I wasn't particularly good at it. But I wanted a car. Having your own wheels meant independence—and independence means everything to teenagers. But I had to learn to drive first.

My mother, anticipating a rerun of her own disheartening experience, nixed my father teaching me to drive. "You're too much alike. You'll kill each other," she told us, as she signed me up for driver's ed.

The place was General George S. Patton Jr. Junior High School in Ft. Leavenworth, Kansas. The car was a 1969 Buick sedan, with four on the floor. The lesson was perfect: I struck up a nice conversation with the driving instructor, Mr. Carlson; I think he really liked me—until I nearly sideswiped a parked MP jeep and Mr. Carlson grabbed his steering wheel, swerved mightily, and missed the jeep with centimeters to spare. No worries; I passed my driving test with flying colors, mainly because, number one, there are very few cars on the road in rural Kansas; number two, Mr. Carlson warned me not to talk during the test. "You can't talk and drive at the same time," he told me.

That's when the Colonel stepped in. Chatterbox that I was, he knew that I needed to master the art of talking and driving. It was a long, protracted battle—and over the course of the next five years I wrecked every vehicle my father owned: the 1967 plum-colored Buick Riviera, the super-cherry black and white 1957 T-bird convertible, the stately aqua 1971 Lincoln Continental, and ultimately, the snazzy silver-green 1974 Ford Maverick, the car my dad gave me when I went to his alma mater, Purdue. Yet, somewhere along the line, the Colonel's advice— "Keep your eyes on the road, goddammit!"—began to sink in. My skill and confidence levels went up, and Dad's insurance rate went down.

By the time I had kids of my own begging for wheels, I was pragmatic enough to let Dad handle their driver's education. We were living in California, where driving a car was mandatory—and dangerous as hell.

Alexis, the eldest, had long before perfected the art of wrapping "Papa Colonel" around her little finger, so the driving lessons went surprisingly well. A serious child who took to the road of life with an earnest caution, she was an excellent driver. Dad rewarded her with a trio of cars. The first was a lemon that shall remain nameless, its only distinction a clutch, which, unlike the Munier women before her, Alexis mastered without a glitch. The second was a 1992 Mercury, with automatic transmission. Mistress of the Clutch, Alexis kept trying to shift the car, tearing up the transmission and limiting her driving direction to forward only. With no reverse, parking became a problem—prompting her grandfather to replace the Mercury with a hot, rebuilt, 1984 Datsun 240Z, which my mother painted with big, bright, Peter Max-style orange flowers. In all, Alexis got three cars out of the Colonel in only two years—a family record that stands to this day.

Greg, the middle child, came of driving age on the heels of his sister. The comedian of the family, Greg was an accident waiting to happen. Reckless and rebellious, he nonetheless surrendered to his grandfather long enough to learn to drive and get his own car, a yellow 1995 Ford Fiesta with air conditioning and automatic transmission. Not content with this, Greg traded the Fiesta in on a more manly, more status-friendly silver 1998 Toyota he bought from a friend's dad's salvage yard. Unfortunately, this macho car had a macho clutch—and it was history within months, leaving Greg without a car. The Colonel did not replace it.

It's been more than fifty years since Dad taught Mom to drive and nearly forty since he taught me. A lot of cars have come and gone in that time. Now, Mom's driving a 2006 Kia Amanti and Dad's racing around in a classic 1989 red Cadillac Allante convertible. (This is what happens when you retire to Las Vegas.) My own 2002 Kia Sportage is in a Massachusetts body shop at the moment, but hey, it wasn't my fault; I got rear-ended. (Seriously. And I wasn't even talking at the time.) Alexis lives in Lausanne, Switzerland, where she and her husband Emmanuel claim not to need a car. (Emmanuel doesn't even know how to drive and doesn't own a driver's license. The Colonel is appalled.) Greg's got a sleek gray 2007 Scion, in which he tools around Los Angeles, mostly with his lovely wife Eliane at the wheel. (It's safer for everyone that way.)

The Colonel's position in our family as the Grand Poobah of Cars has not changed. As I write this, he's teaching my youngest, Mikey, to drive. At sixteen, Mikey is a chip off the old engine block. Like his grandfather, he loves cars, loves driving, loves driving cars fast. The two of them are in heaven, hitting the road in the cool, white 2002 Ford Escort ZX2 coupe that Dad just bought the kid, with the Colonel pontificating on the meaning of cars in a man's life and Mikey listening just long and hard enough to pass the driver's test.

In the next dozen or so years, Elektra, my grandchild and Dad's great-grandchild, will be old enough to drive. You may point out, quite rightly, that she lives in Lausanne and is being raised by two pedestrians in a car-less household in a not-so-car-friendly city in the Swiss Alps.

But the Colonel will change all that.

—*Paula Munier*

# We're Gonna
# Have a Good Time

Whenever I hear Harry Chapin's song, "Cat's in the Cradle"—especially the part when the son asks when his dad is coming home, and the father responds that he doesn't know, "but we'll have a good time then"—tears well up. And the lump in my throat makes it difficult for me to sing along, until the last few lines, when there's a reversal and the aging father finally has time for his son, but the son is busy with his job and his own kids and life. The father understands.

Growing up, I never spent time with my dad one on one. I remember him at meal times, telling stories. I remember him mowing the lawn and tending to his vegetable garden on weekends, taking the family to church every Sunday, going out with Mom every Saturday night, and of course, getting together with extended family on holidays. Once a year, we took our family vacation, too.

But I can recall only one time during my childhood when Dad and I were in a place without Mom and my siblings. In the fourth grade, I was the star of the class play. It meant memorization of line after line, page after page. Mom rehearsed it with me. My teacher, Mrs. Jefferson, marveled at my ability to learn it all so fast. The day of the big production arrived. Scores of parents and grandparents sat in the auditorium/gym to see their children perform minor parts. My mother taught high school and couldn't come. Dad worked as a chemical engineer at Merck. No one would be there for me, and that was all right. I understood and never expected anyone to come to watch me.

At the end of the play, when we took our bows, I peered out into the audience and recognized Dad. Our eyes met; he smiled. As we actors trooped off stage, I remained standing there at the edge, waiting. Dad walked up.

"Good job, Erika. I have to get back to work," he said and turned to leave.

I was dumbfounded. I didn't even realize he knew I was in the play.

I have no other recollection of it being just my dad and me and no one else—not at my graduations, not at my marriage, not at the births of my four kids, not at my mom's funeral. Always, others were around; we were forever part of a family scene.

In 2004, my dad had to have a porcine valve replacement. The surgery was scheduled for early in the morning before my teaching day started. Dad was being operated on by one of the most skilled surgeons at University of North Carolina Hospitals. The night before the procedure, Dad handed me an envelope with information in it as to what I should do about certain things if the operation did not go well and he became incapacitated or worse. We read through his wishes together, seated on the bed in our guest room, and then I put the list in the dresser drawer.

"Dad, when you come back here to recuperate, you can take back your list."

That morning was freezing cold as I drove Dad to the hospital. As he was prepared for surgery, the two of us stayed in a little space divided off by curtains from the next pre-op cubicle. Reassuring doctors and nurses checked in and performed various tasks.

When they came to roll Dad away, I began to well up. "I love you Dad," I told him.

"I know you do," he replied.

"I'll see you in recovery this afternoon."

Dad didn't answer.

I wiped tears from my eyes as I walked fast to my car in the multilevel parking garage across the street. Snow began swirling. As I drove to the middle school, intending to put in a full day of teaching, troubling thoughts raced through my mind.

My brother did not want Dad to have the heart valve replacement, and he had told my sister it was not a good idea. I explained to her that there was not a second choice. In old folks, there is calcification of the aorta and if the opening were to become too narrow, Dad would suddenly keel over dead. My siblings wanted a second opinion. So my physician husband and I took Dad to more cardiologists, who looked at the same pictures and ran the same tests and came to the same conclusion. Dad understood he had to have the operation. So my husband and I arranged it. It was in our hands.

Although classes were cancelled because it was too dangerous for the buses to run, the school was kept open for a teachers' workday. When the work day was over, I returned to the hospital with my husband. We entered the recovery room. There lay my father, attached to tubes and an oxygen mask, unable to communicate except by squeezing my hand.

I talked to Dad but did not ask him questions, because he could not answer. I droned on about my school day, the news, the weather.

After a while, my husband whispered to me, "I think we should go. The nurses have things to do. Tell him we'll be back tomorrow."

I turned to Dad and said, "We're going to go, but I'll be back tomorrow."

His eyes looked frightened, and his grip on my hand tightened.

"Dad, if you want me to stay longer, squeeze my hand as hard as you can."

I was surprised at the strength of an old man who had just had his chest splayed open and a surgeon's hand reached in. I stayed on.

After Dad was released from the hospital several days later, he recovered at my home for one the next few weeks. My sister flew down for one of those weeks and kept him company while I was at work. My daughter still lived at home then and helped entertain Dad during his recovery, and my other grown kids were good about dropping by. Dad did well and returned to his own home within the month. He was eighty-four.

A year later, Dad's memory went into sharp decline. Before two years had passed, we'd sold his house, packed up his belongings, gave much away, and relocated Dad to our guest bedroom. I quit my job.

Now, Dad and I spend long days together alone. Dad is eighty-eight. He has dementia. He chose to live with me. We talk about many things—mostly, his childhood; his working days; his opinions on world events, usually in the past; and of course, the weather.

Dad is a card. He cracks folks up when I take him to the cardiologist, the internist, the dentist, the eye doctor, the barber, the grocery story, the barbecue stand, and on rare occasions, the senior center, where he begrudgingly goes when I insist he get out and do some exercise on machines.

What he likes best is to hang out with me as I go about my daily routine. Often, I think how much I would have loved this special one-on-one attention when I was a child or a teen and really wanted and needed it. Now, I can't get away from it!

As in Chapin's song, our roles have changed.

But unlike the grown-up son in "Cat's in the Cradle," I am not too busy. I don't feel that I have more important things to do than to spend time with Dad. I do have the time, and the desire, to bond with my aging father, even as I age, too. *Better late than never* is an adage I hold true. I'm glad I've had this opportunity. For the first time in my life, I feel like I know my dad. And I can enjoy him now.

My father no longer has the love of his life, the home he was so proud of, the gardens he piddled in, and the status of a breadwinner. No longer does he reside in the state where he was born and raised and lived for eighty-five years. All he has is me, my grown kids, and my husband who works long hours.

I am my father's keeper. I spend quality time with him every day. I am his fifty-six-year-old child, and he is my eighty-eight-year-old daddy. No, we can't throw a ball to each other or hike winding trails or take trips with a camper in tow. But we do crosswords together, watch the news together, eat our meals together, and reflect on people we knew and loved together. Occasionally, we go to Costco and have a Polish sausage, and it makes his day. Simple pleasures.

Yes, we have a good time now. You know we have a good time now.

—*Erika Hoffman*

# Contributors

**Judy L. Adourian** ("The Amazing Powers of Super–Hero Dad") is the owner of Writeyes, a teaching, critiquing, and support network for writers. Her personal essays have appeared in numerous anthologies, including four other *Cup of Comfort*® volumes. Judy is also the Rhode Island Regional Representative for the International Women's Writing Guild.

**Gayle Hauver Baillargeon** ("DIY") operates Petworth Miniatures, a dollhouse shop, out of her home in Winchester, Ontario, Canada, and creates scale buildings and furniture. Her how-to articles are published in *American Miniaturist* magazine. She also paints animal portraits and airbrushes helmets. Gayle and her husband share their country home with three dogs and six cats, and they train Standardbred race horses.

**William M. Barnes** ("Tough Little Dirt Dobber"), a geologist for thirty-five years, began writing at age sixty-five. The author of two novels, *Running on the Edge* and *The White Cockroach*, he is currently working on his third novel, *Nonesuch Boom*. His essays have appeared in various anthologies, including other *Cup of Comfort*® volumes, and he has been published in one book of fictional short stories. He lives in Conroe, Texas, with his wife Margaret.

**Mark Best** ("Being Daddy") lives in Knoxville, Tennessee, with his wife and two children, now twenty-one and sixteen. Whether writing mystery short stories, selling eyeglasses, or managing a jewelry store, Mark's main occupation has been husband and father. He enjoys his job.

**Salvatore Buttaci** ("Papa's Gold Coin") is a retired English teacher who was first published at age sixteen in the *New York News*. His work has been widely published in the United States and abroad. Originally from New Jersey, he lives in West Virginia with his wife Sharon, who continues to inspire him.

**Pedro H. Calves, MD** ("A Few Minutes in the Shade") has been married for over twenty-five years and is the father of a son and a daughter, now sixteen and fourteen. He has worked for ten years as a physician for the chronically and terminally ill on Long Island. "In a world of sadness," he says, "my family anchors my soul to what is important in life."

**Herbert E. Castle** ("You Ain't Doin' Nothin' Anyway") is a technical writer and self-proclaimed grill master who enjoys writing true-life stories about ordinary people's efforts and their extraordinary effects on others. Residing in eastern Kentucky, he and his wife have three children and five grandchildren.

**Samuel P. Clark** ("29 Hours and 37 Minutes," "Entranced," and "To Kayla: With Love, Daddy") is a native Floridian, husband, father of two, and CEO of a social service agency. His stories about the joys and lessons of parent-hood have been published in *The Don't Sweat Stories*, *Blow-Drying the Frog*, *Toddler*, and other anthologies.

**Terri Elders** ("Montana Bananas and Sure Shots") lost her husband, Ken Wilson, to cancer in June 2009. She and his sons planted a tree in his memory in the garden of their retirement home outside Colville, Wash-ington. A retired licensed clinical social worker, Terri serves as a pub-lic member of the Washington State Medical Commission. Her stories have appeared in several publications, including other *Cup of Comfort*® anthologies.

**Barbara Farland** ("Awake") is a prolific creative writer and accomplished business communicator. She credits her success in both arenas to the sup-port of her husband Terry and their quiet home in New Hope, Minnesota. Her work has appeared in *Hugs Bible Reflections for Women*, *Christmas Traditions: True Stories of Holiday Celebration*, and *Minnesota Christian Chronicle*.

**Melissa Gentile** ("Ya Gotta Put a Lotta Love into It"), when not flying by the seat of her pants, can be found teaching high school English and yoga classes in northern New Jersey. She continues to travel to new and dis-tant places and enjoys sharing her experiences with her wonderful family, friends, and students.

**Judy Gerlach** ("Stardust and Paper Moons") works as a personal assis-tant for her husband Greg's video production company in Lexington, Kentucky. Her writing credits include a monologue published by Lillenas Drama as well as two nonfiction stories that appear in Adams Media's *Hero* series. Thanks to her father, Judy has a deep appreciation for jazz music.

**Linda Goldfarb** ("Safety Net") is a writer turned accidental vintner. She, along with her husband Steve, own Anomaly Vineyards, a small cabernet winery in California's Napa Valley. In addition to the winery, Linda keeps busy writing and taking care of her rescue dogs, fifteen-year-old Ashby and three-year-old Danny.

**Cynthia Hamond** ("Turtle Tears") is an award-winning writer whose work has appeared in more than thirty-five publications, including *Woman's World* magazine and the anthology, *Stories for the Heart.* A recurring author for King Features Syndication, she has also written bible study aides and been published by American Greeting Cards. Two of her stories have been made into TV movies. She lives in Minnesota.

**Amy Harold** ("The Old Tin Train") teaches public school on a little island in the Puget Sound and dares to read her poems into a microphone at its one and only library. Her essays and poems have appeared in *El Ojito* and *Ciel Azul.* A mother of three, she writes while others sleep.

**Tea Coiner Harris** ("That's My Daddy!") is a native Oregonian, where she lives near her sister Clare, all their kids, and their father—who moved halfway across the country just to be a daddy. Tea works in fundraising and customer service, and enjoys writing essays as well as stories for children. Her latest book, *Hear the Song of the Fairies,* should be hitting shelves soon.

**Erika Hoffman** ("We're Gonna Have a Good Time") has published over thirty pieces in various anthologies, religious magazines, secular magazines, and newspapers. Her first novel, *Red Flags,* was released in November 2009 (Comfort Publishing).

**Craig Idlebrook** ("Attack of the Killer Ducks") is an instructor for the Boot Camp for New Dads program and a freelance writer in Maine. His work has appeared in more than thirty publications, including *Mothering, Funny Times,* and *Mother Earth News.*

**Sally Jadlow** ("Old Red") serves as a chaplain to corporations in the greater Kansas City area. In her spare time, she teaches writing and poetry to children and adults. She is Grandma to twelve. Here most recent book is *The Late Sooner.*

**Ramona John** ("Act of Atonement") is a retired judge of a juvenile court. Her published works include two books, magazine and newspaper articles, and stories in journals. She lives in Texas with her husband, Dick, and their matronly German shepherd, Greta, and rescue dog, Jake, the mutt who makes them smile.

**Diana Page Jordan** ("My *Real* Dad") reviews books and interviews authors for television, radio, the Internet, and print—including AP Radio Network, XM Satellite, Barnes and Noble's website, and *Open Book with Diana Page Jordan* on Small Plate Radio Network. She also anchors the news in Portland, Oregon, creates podcasts, and presents seminars, and is a voiceover artist and on-camera talent.

**Jolie Kanat** ("Sweeping Effects") is a professional writer based in the San Francisco Bay Area. She is the author of a nonfiction book, *Bittersweet Baby*; a columnist for the *San Francisco Chronicle*; a contributing essayist for several anthologies; a writer for National Public Radio's "Perspectives"; a songwriter for Time Warner and Universal Studios productions; a producer of two CDs for children with special needs; and a creator of greetings cards for Schurmann Fine Papers.

**Sally Kelly-Engeman** ("Caught in Flight") is a freelance writer living in Loveland, Colorado, who has published numerous articles and essays. In addition to reading, researching, and writing, she enjoys ballroom dancing and traveling the world with her husband.

**Libby Kennedy** ("Battle of the Bulging Eyes") lives in Vancouver, British Columbia, Canada, with her two actor kids and her burly, arachnophobe husband Tom. Libby has won numerous prizes for her short fiction and has had several essays published in anthologies. Tom is a twenty-year veteran firefighter with an extensive background in underground mining and search-and-rescue. He used all of his resources and bravery to rescue his precious daughter from the monster spider with the bulging eyes.

**Sandy Keefe** ("A Dad for All Seasons") is a nurse and freelance writer who lives with her husband Ron, daughter Allie, adult daughter Shannon, and grandson Logan in El Dorado Hills, California. Today, Allie is poised on the brink of adulthood and ready to face the world, thanks to the influence of hundreds of people—including her beloved daddy.

**Chynna Tamara Laird** ("A Hero's Welcome") is a psychology student and freelance writer living in Edmonton, Alberta, Canada, with her husband, three daughters, and one son. You'll find her work in many online and in-print parenting, inspirational, Christian, and writing publications. She is most proud of her children's picture book, *I'm Not Weird, I Have SID*, which she wrote for her daughter Jaimie, and her recently released memoir, *Not Just Spirited: Living with Sensory Processing Disorder*.

**Lisa Leshaw** ("The Fruit of a Man's Life") resides in Coram, New York, with her husband of thirty years. A former therapist, she now spends her time writing stories and dreaming up the next great American novel.

**John J. Lesjack** ("Heirlooms") is a retired grade school teacher who lives in Northern California near his son's tomato patch.

**Walter B. Levis** ("Love and Money") was nominated for a 2006 Pushcart Prize and is author of the novel *Moments of Doubt* (2003). His fiction has appeared in a variety of publications, including *North Dakota Quarterly*, the *Amherst Review*, the *Cimarron Review*, and the *Iron Horse Literary Review*.

**Allison Maher** ("Sorry, Dad") is an author and part-time farmer from Aylesford, Nova Scotia, Canada. Her husband of twenty-five years, Dave, still puts up with her antics. Allison has published her first of three young adult novels.

**Kathy L. Adams McIntosh** ("Tattoos of the Heart") balances her time between freelance writing and teaching accounting classes. She publishes fiction stories on chicksandchocolate.com every month and contributed more than thirty articles to the *Community Connection* newspaper before it ceased publication in 2008. She is working on her first novel and lives in Wisconsin with her husband and children.

**Minnette Meador** ("Yes, Sir, Daddy, Darling, Sir!") is an educator, administrator, musician, actress, and writer living in Portland, Oregon. She is the author of the *Starsight* fantasy-adventure novel series; two children's picture books, *A Boy and His Wizard* and *A Boy and His Lizard*; and two historical romance novels, *The Centurion and the Queen* and *The Edge of Honor*. She also contributed an essay to *A Cup of Comfort® for Single Mothers*.

**Paula Munier** ("The Grand Poobah of Cars") is a veteran writer and editor who lives on the South Shore of Massachusetts with her family, two dogs, a 2002 Kia Sportage, and a 2002 Ford Escort ZX2. If she could drive anything she wanted, it would be a vintage Land Rover.

**Hanna R. Neier** ("How to Stop the Rain and Other Small Miracles") grew up with her superhero parents and loving little sister in a quiet suburb outside of Boston, Massachusetts. She is now married to a wonderful man and living in New York City, where she is a practicing attorney.

**Ed Nickum** ("My Life as a Blankie") lives in Cincinnati, Ohio. This is his second story for the *Cup of Comfort®* series. His short humor and horror tales have been published in a dozen print and web-based magazines. He is currently working on a thriller novel tentatively titled *Collecting Angels*.

**Judd Pillot** ("Let's Stop Here, Dad") has written and produced half-hour TV sitcoms for over twenty years, running shows such as *Coach*, *Mad About You*, *Something So Right*, *Just Shoot Me*, *Eight Simple Rules*, and *According to Jim*. He has also written several screenplays, including "Crazy on the Outside," starring Tim Allen and Sigourney Weaver. Before moving to Hollywood from New York, Judd was a documentary filmmaker. But his first love (besides his wife and two boys) is writing prose.

**Jim Poyser** ("Alchemy") lives with his family in Indianapolis, Indiana, where he is the managing editor of the alternative newsweekly, *NUVO*. He writes plays, screenplays, fiction, nonfiction essays, and haiku. With his website, apocadocs.com, he tracks the news of the path of global warming—from the horrific to the hopeful.

**Felice Prager** ("Guys Just Want to Have Fun") is a freelance writer from Scottsdale, Arizona, whose credits include local, national, and international publications. She is also the author of the recently released book *QUIZ IT: ARIZONA.*

**Pete Redington** ("New Dad + Screaming Baby = One Inglorious Spectacle") lives with his wife, son, and their dog in western Massachusetts, where he is an associate of the nonprofit Class Action. He writes about family, dogs, sports, politics, and society. His work has appeared in *The Valley Advocate*, *In These Times*, and *Z Magazine*.

**Kim Rogers** ("Three Precious Words") earned a degree in journalism and public relations from the University of Central Oklahoma. An award-winning freelance writer, her articles have appeared in *Guideposts*, *Sweet 16*, and many other publications. She loves to travel and spent four years in Germany and one year in South Korea, where she taught English. She resides in Oklahoma with her husband and two children.

**Holly Rutchik** ("Even as He Gives His Daughter's Hand") is a personal essayist and stay-at-home mother who recently discovered a love for blogging about her adventures in motherhood. She holds a master's degree in religious studies and much of her writing is in this area. She lives in Wisconsin with her husband Joseph and their daughters Teresa and Anna.

**Suzanne Schryver** ("Drop the Bike") grew up in Williamstown, Massachusetts, gathering nuggets of her father's wisdom. She is a freelance writer of fiction and nonfiction. Her stories have appeared in various anthologies, including other *Cup of Comfort*® volumes. She works in a college writing center and teaches writing online. She lives with her family in New Hampshire.

**Jon Sherman** ("Missing the Game and Other Father's Day Observations") resides in San Clemente, California, with his wife Karin and their two Boston terriers. An avid reader, writer, golfer, and Cub fan, Sherman hopes to publish his first novel in 2010. Or 2011. Or whenever.

**Dayle Allen Shockley** ("What Fathers Do") launched her writing dreams in 1986, with only a notion and a cranky typewriter. Rejection slips poured in, but she persevered. Today, thanks to God's blessings, Dayle is an award-winning writer, author of three books, and contributor to numerous other works. She and her husband live in Texas. They have one grown daughter.

**Alaina Smith** ("Across the Miles") enjoys composing short stories and is a contributor to multiple volumes of two anthology series, *Chocolate for Women* and *A Cup of Comfort*®. She also works part-time as an executive assistant for a theater company and volunteers for progressive causes. She and her husband Frank live near Portland, Oregon.

**Tim Swensen** ("A Mighty Soul") lives in Greenville, Ohio, and serves as an assistant dean at the University of Dayton School of Law. He is married to Krista Lyn Swensen and is the proud father of Abby, Daniel, and Luke. His passion is spending time with this splendid quartet, but he also enjoys reading, writing, and playing tennis.

**Rachel Wallace–Oberle** ("Legacy of Laughter"), a resident of Elmira, Ontario, Canada, has written for numerous publications and agencies, some of which have taken her from the broadcasting booth to the mountains of Haiti. With an education in both journalism and broadcasting, she is one of the founding members of the first Christian radio station in Kitchener, Ontario.

**Bob Walker** ("Father to Son") is a real estate agent who lives with his wife Andrea in Pensacola, Florida. His sons, Kevin and Joey, live in Atlanta with their wives, Anne-Marie and Hollis and their sons Miles and Nathaniel; his daughter Amanda lives in Pensacola. An avid reader, Bob also enjoys politics, golf and swimming.

**Elaine Williams** ("Ain't No Tornado Strong Enough") is a librarian who lives with her husband and daughter in Hillsboro, Ohio. Four days after the tornado that leveled Xenia and destroyed her childhood home, Elaine's father, Ray Kidd, was filmed singing at church for an NBC News broadcast that aired nationwide. In response, people across the country sent letters with donations to help her family rebuild their home.

**Woody Woodburn** ("Being Passed by the Little Fellow Who Follows Me," "Home Is Where the Hero Is," and "Tale of a Kite Without a Tail") is an author and freelance writer residing in Ventura, California. He enjoys running marathons and is very proud to serve on the board of directors for the nonprofit organizations created by his daughter Dallas (WriteOnBooks.org) and son Greg (ShareOurSoles.org).

# About the Author

Colleen Sell has compiled and edited more than thirty volumes of the *Cup of Comfort*® book series. A veteran writer and editor, she has authored, ghost-written, or edited more than 100 books and served as editor-in-chief of two award-winning magazines. She and her husband, T.N. Trudeau, live in a turn-of-the-century farmhouse on a forty-acre pioneer homestead in the Pacific Northwest—a two-hour drive from her wonderful father.